The

Masters' Secrets

of

CRAPPIE FISHING

by John E. Phillips

Larsen's Outdoor Publishing

ISBN 0-936513-29-2

Library of Congress 92-74324

Published by:

LARSEN'S OUTDOOR PUBLISHING
2640 Elizabeth Place
Lakeland, FL 33813
(813) 644-3381

PRINTED IN THE UNITED STATES OF AMERICA

9 10

DEDICATION

"You can give a man a fish and feed him for a day, or you can teach a man to fish and feed him for a lifetime," is an adage not only true about fishing but also about life and people.

John Holley, a friend I met at Livingston University in the mid-60s, fueled my love affair with fishing for crappie year-round. Up until that time, my primary emphasis for crappieing was in the spring during the spawn. Holley took his time and energy and made the effort to teach me to catch crappie year-round. Holley taught me to fish whether the crappie were biting or not.

In college, both Holley and I were young married men, and crappie was our survival food. Holley's tactics not only helped me feed my family then, but the enthusiasm he had and still has for crappie fishing inspires me today. Holley is a good friend and was a patient teacher. This book is dedicated to him.

PREFACE

You can catch more crappie this season than you ever have taken in years past if you understand and practice the secrets of slabology. Slabology is the ability to know where crappie are located, how they are feeding and what is required to make them bite when you want to catch them.

The nation's best slabologists usually can take crappie on any lake under any weather and water condition at any time of the year. They are resourceful and creative and study the haunts, the moods and the feeding patterns of crappie throughout the year to become masters of this sport. A master's degree in slabology requires years of experience to obtain. However, in the mini-course in The Masters' Secrets of Crappie Fishing you can begin to learn the secrets of the crappie fishing masters and then apply them.

ABOUT THE AUTHOR

For more than four decades, John E. Phillips has fished for crappie across the United States, beginning when he barely could toddle along behind his older brother and father. While at Livingston University in West/Central Alabama, the heart of some of the best crappie fishing in the nation, Phillips perfected his techniques and began studying the tactics of the master crappiers he met there.

Phillips also has been a student of crappie as an active outdoor writer and photographer for more than 20 years for both newspapers and magazines. Phillips, the author of 12 outdoor books including: The Masters' Secrets of Turkey Hunting, The Masters' Secrets of Deer Hunting, The Science of Deer Hunting, Doubleday's Turkey Hunter's Bible, Alabama Outdoors Cookbook, How To Make More Profits In Taxidermy, Catch More Crappie, Outdoor Life's Complete Turkey Hunting, Bass Fishing With The Skeeter Pros, North American Hunting Club's Turkey Hunting Tactics, Deer & Fixings and Fish and Fixings, has had more than several hundred articles published on crappie fishing.

An active member of the Outdoor Writers Association of America, the Southeastern Outdoors Press Association, the Alabama Press Association, the Alabama Sportswriters' Association and Outdoors Photographic League, Phillips has won numerous awards for excellence in his magazine and newspaper articles and outdoor books.

Phillips, who feels fortunate to have fished with some of the greatest crappie anglers of our day, brings their knowledge to you in The Masters' Secrets of Crappie Fishing.

CONTENTS

-1-

HOW TO CATCH CRAPPIE
YEAR-ROUND

Are you tired of going fishing and not catching any crappie? Would you like to eliminate some of the guesswork from finding and taking crappie? If such a thing does exist as a crappie guru who knows the secret haunts and specialized techniques that will help you take speckled sides on every outing, how do you find such a man? Do some men have PhD's in catching crappie? The answer is definitely, yes.

Crappie fishing guides and tournament crappie pros must find and take papermouths every day they're on the water. They've unlocked many of the mysteries crappie have held beneath the surface for years. Let's listen as these masters of the sport speak.

PINPOINT THE PATTERNS

Jimmy Brown, of Union City, Tennessee, is a tournament specialist.

"One of the keys to catching more crappie is determining how far the fish are off the bottom. When most anglers look at their depthfinders and see crappie, they want to know how far the crappie are from the surface. However, I've learned that generally no matter at what depth the crappie are from the surface, you consistently can find them at the same depth on the same day when you know the distance they are from the bottom.

Knowing how far the crappie are from the bottom will allow you to catch them more effectively.

"Many guides put out stake beds and brush piles at varying depths for crappie on Kentucky Lake, which is my home lake. Once I learn at what depth the crappie are holding, then I can pinpoint which stake beds to fish. For instance, if I have a stake bed in 10 feet of water, and I spot crappie two feet off the bottom on my depthfinder near that stake bed two feet off the bottom, then I know generally I can expect to locate crappie two feet off the bottom on all my 10 foot deep stake beds. I have found that approximately 80 percent of crappie usually hold at the same level, since crappie will stratify at one water depth.

"If I go to a brush top in 20 feet of water, then I reasonably can expect the crappie to be holding two feet off the bottom there in 18 feet of water. When I check a brushtop in eight feet of water, then the crappie may be at six feet -- two feet off the bottom again. But usually I won't change my fishing as drastically as from 18 feet to six feet.

"Knowing the distance the crappie are from the bottom and determining at what depth the crappie are concentrating in is an example of a pattern within a pattern. By pinpointing what these patterns are, you can catch more fish.

"After I learn crappie are holding around brush at a certain depth from the bottom, then I need to find out how the crappie are positioned in relationship to that cover. If crappie are holding above the brush in one spot, generally they'll be holding above the brush on various brush piles. If the fish are holding off to one side of the brush at one location, then you consistently can locate them off to the side of the brush at other sites.

"However, the position of the crappie on the cover will change at different times of the day. In the summertime, early in the morning and late in the evening, crappie will be close to the surface, because they generally are more shallow in the water during the nighttime than in the daytime. Usually crappie will remain in the position where you locate them for about four hours. Some days they may stay at the same depth of water at the same distance from the bottom and in the same location from the cover all day long. If the day is overcast, the crappie generally will hold their position in the water more consistently all day.

"Yet another critical factor in finding and taking crappie is your ability to effectively work cover. On many days, especially in the spring and summer, crappie will be holding tight to the cover. The way you present the bait to those fish determines whether or not you'll catch them. If you're using heavy lines, heavy sinkers and big corks, often you'll get hung up in the cover and either break off the line or shake the underwater bush, which will disturb the crappie holding there. That's why I use light line and an 11-foot B & M graphite pole. The sensitivity of the pole is the key to being able to feel the structure and work the bait properly.

"With a pole that has a light tip like the B & M, I actually can tell which way a limb is running under the water and work my jig immediately on top of that limb with a tight line. I can bounce the jig along the top of the limb to resemble a feeding baitfish. By being able to tap the cover with the jig, I can tantalize the crappie into biting. By having the sensitivity in the pole and the line, I can feel every twig and limb under the surface, which keeps me from getting hung up.

"Oftentimes crappie fishermen won't put their baits where crappie are in thick cover, because they fear becoming hung. However, if you can feel that jig working through those limbs, you can make the papermouths bite without hanging up.

"To find the most and biggest crappie on any lake, fish the creeks in the center of the lake. Most anglers believe the upper end of a lake warms up before the lower end of a lake does and that the lower end of a lake usually is clearer than the upper end of a lake.

"But my partner and I have learned that the water temperature in the middle of the lake is the most stable, and generally some kind of stain is in the water in that region of a lake. Because the middle of a lake experiences less change than other parts of a lake, my fishing partner and I believe crappie are more stable in the middle of a lake, grow quicker and are less affected by water and weather conditions than in any other section of a lake.

"Next, I look for the proper water depth in the creeks in the middle of a lake. I search for a creek mouth about 30 feet deep. Then I try to locate creek channels that drop off from 10 feet to 18 feet deep, which will be natural highways for the crappie to use. During the spawn and in warm weather, the crappie can move into the shallow water to spawn and then swim back to that 10- or 18-foot water when a cold front hits or when the fish have completed spawning. These kinds of creeks are ones baitfish like to travel also.

"Another critical ingredient my partner and I look for after we locate a creek in the middle of a lake that has the characteristics we require to fish for crappie is to choose the creek with the most underwater bends in its creek channel. Crappie generally will hold on the outside bends of these underwater creek channels, which is an example of the type of pattern we attempt to pinpoint.

"Too, we fish in the middles of the creeks on these creek channels and bends because most people don't fish in those regions. Most crappie fishermen hunt cover around the bank and fish the cover related to the bank. Consequently, bank-bound crappie will be harvested the heaviest. Also, the chances of your catching a big crappie are not as good close to a bank, since so many people are fishing that area. However, when you fish the underwater structure out in the middle of a creek where the underwater creek channels are, you'll usually catch more and bigger crappie."

10

Wherever the crappie are positioned in relationship to the brush is where they usually will be holding, regardless of where the brush pile is located.

SEARCH FOR STRUCTURE

Roger Gant of Corinth, Mississippi, has his own guide business on Pickwick Lake on the Mississippi/Tennessee/ Alabama borders and has fished the Crappiethon Classic for two years.

"I believe one of the main secrets to catching more crappie is understanding water clarity and knowing how to find structure on the bottom. If I go to a new lake, I search for structure where crappie should be holding according to the water temperature and the time of the year. Not much structure is in the water at Pickwick Lake. Unless the water is stained, crappie may spawn as deep as 20 feet there. I've caught crappie from 26 feet to 30 feet deep in the spring and summer on Pickwick.

"To get a small jig down that deep to catch spawning crappie, generally I troll a small diameter line like Stren's Magnathin six-pound test line on B & M's graphite crappie poles. But if the water is dingy, I may fish with eight-pound test. In clear water, I'll troll two, 1/8-ounce jigs tied about 16 inches apart over structure. If the water is very clear, I troll particularly slow.

Roger Gant of Corinth, Mississippi, consistently catches stringers of crappie like this because he knows where, how and when to find them.

"Also, I troll in the middle of a lake to catch crappie. When you're fishing in water deeper than 20 feet, crappie don't have to hold on ledges and drop-offs. I look for stump fields in that deep water, because usually crappie will be in those types of regions. I've found that crappie generally will associate with any kind of irregular bottom -- whether it's a stump field, a drop-off or a hump out in the middle of a lake. I believe large crappie prefer deep water. I catch crappie all year long in deep water."

SET OUT FISH ATTRACTORS

"If you want to catch crappie under various water and weather conditions every day of the year, then you have to put out habitat in which crappie can hold," says Steve McCadams of Paris, Tennessee, who is a fulltime crappie fishing guide of Kentucky/Barkley lakes. "I place treetops, stake beds, willow trees and brush in the water to bring the crappie and the fisherman closer together. By sinking habitat

Steve McCadams of Paris, Tennessee, is a crappie fishing guide who studies the fish and their habits.

in old reservoirs, you actually can improve the crappie fishing, because much of the original cover may be gone.

"Although no place is a bad spot for building a brush pile, some sites do produce more crappie than others. The more cover you sink for crappie, the more crappie you'll be able to catch. I sink cover in several different depths and let the crappie decide where they prefer to be. Crappie will be in the shallow water cover when spawning time is near. If the spawn is on, and the lake level drops drastically, the fish will move to deeper cover. By having cover sunk at three different depths in the same area, generally you can locate fish at any time of the year.

"For instance, I may sink brush in eight feet of water besides sinking another pile of brush in 12 feet of water and yet another in 18 feet of water in that same general location. Then, no matter the time of the year or what the weather and water conditions are, the crappie in that area have brush on which to hold and relate."

STUDY THE WEATHER

Dave Clark of Lincoln, North Carolina, is another crappie tournament pro.

"I'm convinced barometric pressure and weather determine where the crappie will be and how they will bite. Just ahead of a cold front, crappie usually will bite better. But

13

when a high front moves through after a cold front, perhaps a crappie's balance may be off somewhat, and the fish tend not to bite as well. Generally the crappie will go into the deeper water and hold up against the brush. Maybe the fish are attempting to stabilize themselves in the water.

"If that cold front hits during the spawn, crappie will move out into the deeper water and hold in the places where you found them during the pre-spawn and often where they'll be in the post-spawn -- in about eight to 10 feet of water. One of the best baits to use at this time of the year during a cold weather front is minnows, since minnows will move in the brush without your actually having to move them.

"If I'm fishing jigs, I'll cast a 1/32-ounce jig in close to the cover and retrieve it slowly on a spinning reel mounted on my B & M graphite rod. As the line on the reel comes back, I allow the line to just barely touch my index finger, which causes the jig to twitch just a little as it's being retrieved. I think that erratic motion, although small, gives the jig a more life-like action and will make tight-lipped crappie bite. Generally, I fish 1/32-ounce jigs year-round, because I have more faith in the tiny jigs than in the bigger jigs.

"I like a 4-1/2-foot to five foot B & M rod with four pound test line, because I can cast the jigs further using this pound test line and this light action rod than I can with heavier tackle. I also utilize a Color-C-Lector to determine the color of jigs I should be casting, especially when I'm fishing in water less than 25 feet deep. If I want to catch very big crappie, I usually will fish in 25 feet to 30 feet of water. Although crappie are harder to catch in that deeper water, generally the crappie I take are the larger fish.

"Since I realize jigs are more difficult to see at that depth because of light penetration, when I'm fishing deep, I generally fish a chartreuse jig, which I think can be seen by the crappie at greater depths. In clear water, I prefer light-colored jigs like tan and white, yellow and white or even smoke-colored or transparent jigs. If the water is stained, I'll choose either chartreuse, red and chartreuse and/or black and chartreuse or maybe even orange with a yellow tail. Matching the water condition and water depth to the color of jig you fish is very important if you want to catch more and bigger crappie."

- 2 -

HOW TO TAKE
WINTERTIME CRAPPIE

Wintertime crappie fishing can be highly productive with plenty of fast action and big fish. Or, icy weather crappieing can be as slow as pouring maple syrup out of a cold pot on a frosty morning. What makes the difference is where you find the crappie. Let's look at some ideal wintertime crappie situations.

Gene Parker, an angler on Lake Eufaula in Alabama, explains, "If anglers are on Lake Eufaula at the right time during the winter, then they can catch all the crappie they want. Since a National Wildlife Refuge is situated along the banks of Lake Eufaula, each year several thousand acres of the refuge are flooded to provide a home for wintering waterfowl.

"When the waterfowl season is over, these man-made ponds are pumped out. The water from these duck ponds is pumped back into Lake Eufaula. Then the ponds will dry up for the spring planting of corn and other grains to feed the ducks and geese through the winter.

"The water from these shallow water ponds usually is much warmer than the wintertime water in Lake Eufaula. When the water is pumped out of the ponds and poured back into the lake, plenty of warm water comes into a big area of cold water. That warm water being pumped into the lake draws crappie like a magnet.

If you know where to find wintertime crappie, the fishing can be fantastic.

"Within only a few hours after the pumps start running, the crappie begin to show up in large numbers at these sites. Most of the time these winter crappie will be big fish. Because they are in such a confined area of warm water, they are easy to catch. I've seen two anglers fish half a day and catch a limit of crappie that weighs between 1/2-pound and two pounds each.

"There's no doubt that if you crappie fish on Eufaula when the duck ponds are being pumped out in the wintertime, you can load up your cooler. Usually, the fishing is so fast, and the crappie are so aggressive that jig fishing seems to be the best. The weather may be cold, but the crappie fishing can be hot."

READ THE WEATHER TO CATCH MORE CRAPPIE

The time was the end of November when most of the major colleges were playing their last football games of the season. A warm front had come through where we lived. For two or three days, the weather had been pleasant. But the TV weatherman was predicting that a major winter storm would hit before nightfall.

My brother and I had been fishing a shallow water beaver pond off a major river system with numbers of cypress trees growing in it. Because the pond was more shallow than the river, the water in the beaver pond was warmer than the river water. Therefore, the crappie were more active.

You, too, can take more cold weather crappie if you can find beaver ponds, cut-offs, sloughs, coves and/or bays of major river systems that normally hold crappie during the winter months. Then, when there is a warm spell, that water will warm up quicker than the river water. The crappie often will move into these shallow pockets and hold on submerged trees, stumps and/or the roots of live trees.

Although my brother and I had found the fishing to be very good all along during those warmer winter days, about five hours before the front was due to come in, the crappie went on a feeding spree. The reason was simple. We were in a warm water area just ahead of a front.

As most sportsmen know -- both fish and animals tend to feed more aggressively ahead of a front. Since we were in a region where the crappie already were concentrated just before the front hit, we were able to catch the most and some of the biggest crappie we ever had taken. The front was fast-moving. As soon as we felt the temperature drop only slightly, the crappie quit biting.

LOCATE THE THERMOCLINE

During the winter months, many lakes turn over, which means the coldest water will be on the top, and the warmest

The author, John Phillips, has located his share of wintertime crappie by learning how to search for them in warm water.

water will be on the bottom. This condition is unlike the summertime when the warmer water is on the top, and the colder water is on the bottom.

Because crappie seek a comfort zone, often they will be looking for that warmer, deeper water. But usually the slabs prefer some type of cover to hide in and hold on so they can attack baitfish. To pattern wintertime crappie, anglers must look for cover along the thermocline where crappie can hole up. In many lakes and rivers, this cover may be on the edges of old creek and river channels and along stump rows where the warmer water is close to the bottom.

Remember that during the extreme cold of the winter months, the crappie's body metabolism slows down. The fish will not chase a bait as far as it will in the spring and summer. The crappie angler has to fish his bait slow and deep to get bites.

Although trolling usually is not thought to be a slow method of angling, actually it can be as slow as drop-fishing. On Kentucky Lake in the dead of winter, many crappie anglers troll for crappie using crappie rigs with two minnows on them along underwater creek and river channels.

Most anglers generally consider trolling a technique for catching bass or saltwater fish like sailfish and marlin, and in both of these types of trolling, the boat moves forward faster than what is required to troll for crappie. If you watch an effective crappie fisherman trolling in the wintertime, you may not be able to tell that his boat is moving. As one crappie guide says, "The slower you go, the more fish you catch."

A more descriptive term for wintertime crappie trolling may be bumping.

"I hit the trolling motor just enough to make the boat move slightly," this same crappier explains. "When the boat comes to a full stop, my fishing partner or I will bump the motor again just to make the boat move forward one to 1-1/2 feet. Using this slow, trolling method, we are dragging the minnows right in front of the crappie's nose. If the fish is there, it will take the bait. If we catch a fish, we attempt to stay in the same area and troll back and forth with our minnows to take more crappie out of the school."

On Lake Purdy near Birmingham, Alabama, wintertime crappie fishermen troll the creek and river channels using jigs and very light line -- two- to four- pound test. Although these sportsmen move slowly and fish deep, they do catch crappie.

USE A DEPTHFINDER

In Texas, Bryan Duplechain catches plenty of big, fat, wintertime crappie in 30 to 40 feet of water near the dam at Lake Fork Reservoir fishing minnows on humps and creek channels.

"I think winter is the best time to catch crappie," Duplechain says. "I know exactly where the crappie must be on this particular lake, because the crappie are searching for bottom breaks where there's plenty of oxygen in deep water and the water temperature is comfortable for them. With a depthfinder, these deep water crappie are easier to locate and catch than at other times of the year, because I usually find them in large schools."

CAST FOR WINTERTIME CRAPPIE

If an angler has studied deep water structure and knows where stump rows and old creek channels usually home good schools of crappie, he can fish these areas by casting and retrieving in the winter. Elbert Parker, a guide on Lake Weiss on the Alabama/Georgia border, is probably one of the best wintertime crappie fishermen I have ever have met. Parker is not a shoreline angler but fishes open water. He knows where plenty of brush, stumps and underwater structure are in the middle of the lake.

"During the wintertime, those crappie get down in and under the stumps and the stumps' roots along the old river and creek channels," Parker mentions. "Many times these fish won't show up on a depthfinder because they are holding under the stumps and the roots. The only way you can discover the crappie are there is to fish for them.

"Crappie hit very lightly in the wintertime. You must be able to see your line as the jig falls, since the papermouths often will take the jig on the fall. Unless you see that light strike, you can miss the fish. However, if the crappie don't take the jig on the fall, then I use a slow, easy retrieve -- trying to bump the cover without getting hung on it. But I expect to lose jigs when I fish in the winter. If you're not losing jigs, then you're not fishing where the crappie are."

I went crappie fishing with Parker a couple of years ago on a winter's day when an ice storm hit. My rainsuit had ice on the back of it. Occasionally, Parker and I had to dip our rods in the water to keep the guides from freezing up. However, after angling eight or 10 different locations in the middle of the lake, we caught a limit of crappie by fishing slow and deep and breaking off plenty of jigs.

According to Parker, "When you are wintertime crappie fishing, you've gotta fish rough stuff. You have to have your

An effective rig to use for trolling for crappie is to put a slip sinker up the line stopped by a piece of shot lead and a hook and minnow below the lead. Using this tactic, if the hook gets hung because the lead is above the hook when the line is lowered, the lead often will pull the hook out of the cover.

jigs in the thick cover. If you are not prepared to lose 50 jigs a day, then you shouldn't plan to fish for cold weather crappie."

USE CONCRETE SOLUTIONS TO EARLY CRAPPIE

Most of us believe that crappie season begins with the announcement of spring when the woods appear as though they are covered with snow from the white blossoms of the dogwoods. I always have felt that proper crappie attire is tennis shoes with no socks, cut-off bluejeans, a t-shirt and a baseball cap.

But today I was in warm hunting boots and a snowmobile suit worn over a heavy pair of jeans, a wool shirt and thermal underwear. My Coleman catalytic heater provided the warmth I needed to relieve the aching in my fingers. Every now and

Concrete structures like bridges are productive wintertime habitat for crappie.

then I stirred the water in the minnow bucket just to make sure it didn't freeze.

Deer season had been over for about a month, while turkey season had not yet begun. For the last two weeks, I had been wanting to catch a mess of fresh crappie for the skillet. Although I realized I was some weeks away from the big spring crappie run, when you want to catch crappie, whether or not the time of year is right doesn't really matter.

My partner, Joe Alexander, and I already had angled several downed treetops and a good line of standing timber. Although we had taken about 15 crappie, none of them were larger than three fingers. I would have been ashamed to put those small papermouths in the livewell, let alone the skillet.

As we moved from one portion of the river to the other, we passed under a railroad trestle, the columns of which were facing the sun. We decided to test the water to see if there were some crappie in the region. Alexander and I set our corks at different depths and began to drop-fish next to the piling.

Quick as my quill cork straightened up on the water, it sank. I set the hook, and the pole arched like a question mark. The fish was fighting so hard that at first I thought I might have caught a largemouth or a white bass that was holding close to the structure. But as the pole flexed its muscle, I saw the wide, white, speckled sides of a fat, early season crappie catch the rays of the sun as the fish darted back for the deep. Once again I muscled the pole, the bamboo responded, and the crappie came to the surface. The fish weighed over a pound and was the first keeper we had caught.

After rebaiting quickly, once more my cork never stood up in the water but sank as soon as the line was taut. The crappie were holding in about four feet of water. Soon my partner shallowed up his cork and started catching fish. We boated about 15 crappie before the action waned. We fished a few other pilings that were in the shade but quickly decided that the pilings that faced the sun on this particular day produced the most crappie.

Like many anglers, I have found that crappie can be patterned just like bass. Once you locate the type of structure the crappie like to hold on, then if you can find that same kind of structure in another area, you reasonably can assume that crappie should be holding on that structure similar to the way they were holding on the structure you originally fished.

Alexander and I left the trestle, went upriver and found a highway bridge where the pilings faced the sun. Once more we took crappie in about five feet of water. We made two more stops that day and caught slabs off all the concrete structure we encountered that faced the sun. At lunchtime, we went back to our first trestle, caught 10 more crappie and began to run our concrete pattern again. But in the after-noon, we seemed to catch more crappie on the opposite side of the pilings than we had in the morning. Apparently, the fish were following the sun. As the concrete heated up, the water was warmed. The fish chose the warmer water over the colder water every time.

WHY CONCRETE ATTRACTS CRAPPIE

In cold weather, large concrete structures like bridge abutments, wingwalls of locks and dams and railroad trestles absorb heat and then transfer that heat into the water to supply a comfortable environment for early season crappie. Crappie move to creek channels, river channels and ledges to feed and find a warmer environment at those places when the water is cool. Most bridges and trestles have at least one concrete column just on the edge of an old creek or river channel that they cross. Naturally, as crappie migrate up and down that creek or river channel, they find the warm water the concrete piling has caused and locate the baitfish that are holding on that piling for warmth and food.

The fish will tend to congregate on these particular pilings. Although crappie will be on pilings further away from the creek channel, usually the pilings closest to the creek channel homes the best crappie fishing during the colder months.

But most of the crappie will be holding on the calm water side of these concrete structures. Once again the fish will come to these areas for two reasons -- the water is warmer, and the baitfish are more abundant. One of the most successful spots that I ever have found to catch early season crappie is at the end of a wingwall. Crappie may be holding on the calm water side at the end of a wingwall so they can rest and feed out of the current. The current washing around the corner of the wingwall will sweep food right into the fish's mouth. Sometimes an angler can limit out fishing this type of concrete structure.

Property owners may build small concrete walls or utilize broken pieces of concrete to break up the currents near their lake or river homes. This broken concrete still has its heat absorbing properties and provides a home for the microscopic organisms the baitfish like to eat. I have found some productive crappie hotspots on the backsides of concrete structures and rip-rap made of concrete. Although crappie will come to concrete for warmth and to feed, usually they will not fight the current to stay warm and get a full belly of baitfish. The largest number of crappie regularly will be taken on the calm water side or the ends of the concrete structure where the water is not as swift.

HOW TO ADD SPICE TO CONCRETE

Crappie prefer to have structure they can get into like limbs, logs and brush. The disadvantage to concrete fish attractors is they don't have hiding places for crappie. However, some resourceful anglers have remedied this problem by sinking brush next to the concrete to further enhance the structure's fish-attracting properties. Sinking the brush on the backside of the current is a must so the concrete structure will break the current and keep the brush from being washed away.

CATCHING CONCRETE CRAPPIE

Crappie position themselves on concrete structures at different depths at various times of the year. Either of two techniques can tell an angler at what depth the crappie are holding. Motor your boat along the edge of the concrete while reading your depthfinder, which may allow you to see the crappie and determine at what depth they are staying. However, many times the crappie will be holding so close to the structure you won't be able to spot them on the depthfinder.

But the problem with locating crappie by reading your depthfinder while motoring your boat along the edge of the concrete is, if the fish are shallow I believe they can be spooked by being run over with a boat. So I start off by assuming that the crappie are holding shallow on the concrete.

If I am jig fishing, I anchor my boat upstream of a piling. I cast downstream, letting my jig fall right beside the concrete piling. On each cast, I count my jig down and then begin to retrieve. The first cast and retrieve will be right below the surface of the water, because often on a bright, warm day -- even in cold weather -- crappie may be only a foot or two under the surface. With each successive cast, I allow the jig to drop from six inches to a foot deeper than the cast before, retrieving it to the boat with a steady retrieve. When a fish strikes, I continue to fish that depth of water to try and take more slabs.

Shown is the author with a good morning's catch of wintertime crappie.

Another important ingredient in taking concrete crappie is to keep the jig bumping the concrete as long as possible during the retrieve. Many times a papermouth will take the bait just as it leaves the end of a concrete structure. As long as your jigs are in contact with the concrete, you will catch more crappie than if the jigs are swimming in open water two or three inches from the concrete.

Concrete crappie are not unlike fish found on other types of structure during this time of year. They soon will wise up to the color of the jig you're throwing and quit biting. But by changing the color of the jig when the crappie stop hitting the lure, often you can keep on taking crappie.

Of course, there are some concrete crappie that are fickle. You may cast every color of jig in your tackle box without the crappie taking the bait, until you find the exact color they want on that specific day. Sometimes that color may be an unusual color of grub like orange, pink or blue and white stripe. But once you discover the particular color the fish will hit, you may limit out on fat slabs.

When fishing live bait, I have found that keeping the minnow in contact with the concrete will pay off in more bites. Anchoring your boat out either a pole or a rod's length from the structure may be the most productive tactic. Setting your cork or fishing a tight line at various depths will allow the angler to determine at what depth the crappie are feeding. Once you start getting bites, then change all your lines so the baits will be placed at the depth where the crappie seem to be holding. If there is a current running, let your cork bump the concrete so the bait will be washed down the side of the structure and into the eddy hole to trigger strikes.

One of the best live bait fishermen I ever have angled with, Tom Adams, has a theory about live bait. "I believe on certain days crappie prefer one size of bait over another size. Although some days they want a small minnow, on other days they like a large minnow. I have found that crappie become accustomed to feeding on the size of bait that is the most prevalent on the structure where they're holding. If most of the baitfish holding on the concrete structure are small and the crappie are used to eating that small bait, then perhaps the crappie will be more likely to take a small minnow than a big minnow. If the baitfish on that structure are large, and the crappie feed on the big baits, than an angler naturally can assume that larger minnows will produce more crappie in that area than smaller minnows will. But there is no sure way of knowing until you start fishing.

"When I go out for a day of fishing, I carry a bucket of small minnows and a bucket of large minnows and experiment with both to see which size of bait the crappie prefer. If I catch more crappie on small minnows, then I only utilize small minnows until I use up all of the bait I have. When I run out of small minnows, I will try to fish the large minnows. However, if I find that the crappie are turning down the larger bait, I leave the structure and return to the bait shop to buy more small minnows.

"I think that not giving the crappie the size of bait they prefer is a mistake many crappie fishermen make. My time is better spent by going back to the bait shop to purchase the size of minnows the fish are biting that day than to try to convince the crappie holding on the concrete structure to bite a bait bigger than what they want. This principle applies to larger minnows as well as small minnows. If the crappie prove they favor the bigger minnows, I don't try to persuade the fish to take small minnows. After the fish tell me what bait they want to bite, I try to provide it."

WHEN IS THE BEST TIME TO ANGLE CONCRETE ATTRACTORS

There is really only one bad time for catching crappie around concrete -- in the middle of the summer on a bright day when the concrete is hot enough to fry eggs.I'm sure there are some outdoorsmen who do take crappie under these conditions. However, they will catch more crappie if they fish that same concrete structure at night in the summer.

No matter how productive a concrete structure is, how well it is positioned, and how many crappie it is capable of holding, no structure -- concrete or not -- always will concentrate crappie at all times of the year under all weather and water conditions. All of us have fished bridge pilings and railroad trestles before, limited out on slabs easily and quickly one day and then not had a bite on that same concrete structure for the next three days. There is no such thing as a piece of structure that always will hold and produce plenty of crappie for the skillet.

However, when I am out crappie fishing, I never pass by a large piece of concrete in the winter that I don't cast a jig to it or drop a minnow around it. When the weather is cool and the crappie are hunting warm water, concrete structures are a good place to look for hot slab action.

- 3 -

HOW TO ICE FISH FOR CRAPPIE

Because not much ice fishing exists in my hometown of Birmingham, Alabama, the first time I went to Iowa and sat all day on a five-gallon bucket and jiggled a little ice fly through a hole for fish I couldn't see, I was bored to tears. Also my back quickly got out of joint.

However, when I went to Lake Mille Lacs in Minnesota to test Berkley's new ice fishing line and their new Northern Light rods in the middle of the winter, I gained a respect for the fun found in ice fishing. Now I'm almost ready to give up my bass boat and move north to build an ice house on the lake.

My new-found enthusiasm came from fishing a day with Dave Genz, a resident of Minneapolis, Minnesota, and the president of Ice Fishing Systems, who completely revolutionalized ice fishing for me.

"After fishing on the ice for 43 years, I decided a better way to catch panfish like bluegills and crappie through the ice must exist," Genz recalled. "In the summertime, I could move all around the lake in my boat and go from spot to spot finding fish. But during the winter months, I was stuck in one place in an icehouse."

Because of his discontent, Genz has designed and built a portable icehouse he can pull behind him as he walks across the frozen lakes and has developed an Ice Box which sits on the ice, carries a motorcycle battery and a Hondex FL8 flasher, all of which are essential keys to finding and catching

Dave Genz of Minneapolis, Minnesota, a master of ice fishing, consistently catches crappie on frozen lakes and rivers.

more panfish through the ice. After Genz drills a number of holes in the ice, he moves the Ice Box from hole to hole until he finds fish with his depthfinder.

But the key to Genz's style of fishing is the sensitivity of the depthfinder he uses. The Hondex flasher shows fish in three different colors -- green, orange and red. The color

Inside an icehouse anglers like Louie Stout of Bristol, Indiana, pictured here, can watch their depthfinders and not only see the baits but also their jigs.

green denotes small fish, orange means the fish are larger, and red shows the largest fish.

However, what amazed me the most was that I could observe a 1/32-ounce ice fly fall from the surface of the water to a depth of 33 feet on the flasher. Not only could I see the ice fly on the screen of the flasher, but I also could watch the fish move in to take the bait. I had my own video game inside my icehouse.

If I saw a little crappie coming toward my bait, I could move my ice fly away from the small fish and either up or down to where a bigger crappie could take the lure. If I spotted a crappie moving toward my bait and saw the red line representing the fish overlap the green line which was my ice fly, I knew the fish had taken the bait, and I should set the hook. From watching the depthfinder, I could see a strike on the flasher before I ever felt the bite on my line. Something else I learned from the flasher was that I could determine whether the fish were in an aggressive feeding mode or in a non-feeding mode. An active fish would follow my ice fly up toward the surface to attack, but an inactive fish would not move a foot or two to take the bait. When I saw that the crappie were inactive on the flasher, I would put my ice fly tipped with a Eurolarva (a maggot) in front of the fish and shake the bait until the fish hit.

According to Genz, "To get the maximum amount of sensitivity from the transducer, I use a bracket that sticks out of the Ice Box and allows me to move the head of the transducer until it is perfectly level. To further insure the transducer is level, I utilize a stick-on bubble level that can be acquired at almost any hardware store. Once I have the bubble in the center of the level, I know my transducer is shooting the signals straight to the bottom, which means I can obtain maximum sensitivity with the sensitivity set from one to 1-1/2."

Genz's portable icehouse also featured a small Coleman lantern, which provided light and made my fishing hut warm and comfortable. The Hondex depthfinder was more like a video game than the machines found at an arcade. This new style of ice fishing taught me much about how crappie feed and move under the ice.

However, with this type of video game, instead of bells and whistles going off when you win, you get to bring a fat crappie to the surface to take home to supper. I may be from the South, but I've learned how to enjoy and appreciate northern ice fishing.

- 4 -

HOW TO CATCH PRE-SPAWN CRAPPIE

Some of the biggest crappie of the year are caught just prior to the spawn because, not only are the female crappie full of roe, but often they are still carrying their winter weights. Since pre-spawn crappie can be in various places at different times of the year in reservoirs throughout the country, any writer who tells you exactly where to look for pre-spawn crappie more than likely is talking about where to search for them on the lakes and rivers he knows. Here are some examples of where and how I have found pre-spawn crappie in the past, and where you may search for them at this time of year.

DISCHARGE CRAPPIE

In late February in North Georgia, the weather is still cool, but the big, slab crappie often will spawn about the second or third week in March, as in many other parts of the country. Three to four weeks before the spawn, these fish usually are hunting warmer and more shallow water in preparation for the spawn.

A friend of mine, Robert Holland, had found a small stream that was used by a major factory near Rome, Georgia, to dump warm water discharge. The stream flowed into a nearby river that had plenty of crappie in it.

"I've seen some folks fishing down by the bridge, and they had some pretty nice-sized crappie," Holland told me one day.

Since the stream was not very far from either of our jobs, we decided to give it a try one afternoon after work. Using jigs and corks, we cast out into the warm water and let our jigs wash downstream. After taking about eight or 10 crappie that afternoon, I decided to move further down the bank to see if I could locate a better place to fish.

I noticed a narrow point jutting out into the current and forming an eddy pool on the backside of the point. I cast my jig out and allowed the cork to carry the jig around the point and into the eddy hole where the cork sank. My rod bowed, my line sang, and I brought a fat, 1-1/2-pound crappie to the bank. Quickly unhooking the fish, I threw out again -- letting the cork drift the jig into the same eddy hole. Once more the cork sank, and I took a nice crappie.

After I had put my 15th fish on the stringer, Holland yelled out from upstream, "Hey, John. You catching any fish? These up here have just about quit biting."

"Yeah, I'm catching a few," I replied, trying to sound unexcited.

In a few minutes, Holland came down the bank, pulled up my stringer, and said, "Golly, why didn't you tell me you were catching these kinds of crappie?"

Barely managing to keep a straight face, I explained that I wasn't really sure how good the place was where I was fishing and that I wanted to be certain there were plenty of crappie there before I told Holland to move down and fish with me.

Holland, who recognized a lie when he heard one, told me to, "Move over boy. I'm gonna catch me some of those slabs."

Anywhere you can find warm water discharge in small creeks and streams that run into major reservoirs, often you will locate a honey hole for big, pre-spawn crappie.

DITCH CRAPPIE

On major reservoirs, crappie that are preparing to spawn generally will run up creek and river channels and wait for the warm weather and the correct water temperature to move out

Sam Heaton of Gadsden, Alabama, is a guide on Weiss Lake, which is known as the Crappie Capital of the World. He consistently catches big crappie just prior to the spawn.

on the flats to spawn. Often a hole or a deep spot at the very end of a ditch or a small creek channel will be where large schools of big crappie will hold just prior to the spawn.

"During the pre-spawn and post-spawn times of the year, I usually can find crappie ganged-up along ditches and the backs of little creek channels," Charlie Ingram, a fishing guide with Tom Mann's Fish World Guide Service on Alabama's Lake Eufaula, explained. "Many times in the backs of these little ditches, I can sit in one spot and limit out on crappie. If there is any cover at all in these holes, you can expect to locate numbers of crappie. Any place you can find a ditch, a cut or a small secondary creek channel close to a spawning area, you can expect to discover crappie. Most of the time these crappie will be very aggressive because they are trying to feed up ahead of the spawn. Although most

35

Charlie Ingram of Eufaula, Alabama, likes the 3/4-ounce Jack Chancellor or Hopkins jigging spoon to catch big, pre-spawn crappie.

anglers think that during the spawn is the best time to catch big crappie, I've learned that the pre-spawn is when I find and catch the most large crappie.

"To be an effective pre-spawn fisherman, you must be able to read a depthfinder and a topo map. The topo map will tell you where the small ditches, secondary creeks, and little cuts are in the lake's bottom. The depthfinder will help you get on this structure and show you the cover and the fish holding there.

"During the pre-spawn, I personally prefer to fish either the 3/4-ounce Jack Chancellor or Hopkins jigging spoon because I can angle vertically with it. It's a big spoon and produces large crappie. Because of the jigging spoon's weight, if I get tangled in cover, I can shake it free."

STUMP CRAPPIE

One of the best pre-spawn crappie fishermen I ever have known is Nolen Shivers of Birmingham, Alabama. During the spring and summer, Shivers is an avid bass fisherman. How-

36

ever, during the fall, winter and pre-spawn time, he is an enthusiastic crappie fisherman.

According to Shivers, "I can catch more crappie in the cold months than I can bass. I think that catching any kind of fish is a lot better than not taking fish. Besides, I like to eat crappie. During the pre-spawn, I catch some of the finest crappie that can be taken all year long."

Shivers has two basic techniques for taking pre-spawn crappie. He fishes shallow, underwater stumps along creek and river channels that are often 20 to 30 yards from the bank or brush shelters under docks.

"I've found that crappie come up out of the deep water and hold on underwater stumps along creek and river channels in six to 10 feet of water waiting on the right water temperature to move into the bank to spawn," Shivers reported. "Even when the crappie do spawn, the stumps are more productive than the banks. The crappie that are moving to the banks hold on the stumps before they go to the bank. Also, the crappie that are coming away from the bank after they spawn hold on the stumps before they swim out to deep water."

If you can find underwater stumprows along or near an old creek channel close to a spawning area, your chances are good for locating and taking crappie.

DOCK CRAPPIE

In Shivers' other pre-spawn technique, he fishes docks.

"Remember that most lake and river residents who have docks usually build some kind of brush shelter or put some structure out in front of their docks so they can come down and sit on their docks and catch fish," Shivers commented. "Most of the time the brush will be about a canepole's distance or a little further from the dock. Having a depthfinder will pay off for you. By motoring your boat back and forth in front of the dock, you usually can find this sunken cover on your depthfinder. The crappie will move into this type of structure during the pre-spawn because it gives them cover to hold on while they're waiting on the temperature to warm up.

"If there's no cover in front of a dock, then I assume the cover is under the dock. Oftentimes a dock owner will sink the cover under the dock to keep the fish close to his pier. If you cast light jigs up under the dock, you can catch crappie."

FEEDER CREEK CRAPPIE

Another productive place to look for crappie during the pre-spawn is in the mouths of feeder creeks. Many times large schools of crappie will move out of a river channel and hold in mid-water in the mouth of a creek. The fish may be positioned there because the water generally is somewhat warmer than the water found on the river channel, and there are numbers of baitfish, too. By holding in the mouths of creeks, as soon as that creek water starts to warm up enough to trigger the spawn, the crappie will be ready to move up the creek channel and onto the spawning areas.

There are several methods to use to catch these creek mouth crappie. Most anglers prefer to troll in the mouths of creeks using 1/24- and 1/32-ounce jigs on two and four-pound test line. When you are trolling the open water and you do not have to worry about losing crappie in thick cover, then you can fish the lighter line. The smaller the diameter of the line, the faster and deeper it will allow the crappie jig to sink. To troll a 1/32-ounce jig eight to 10 feet under the surface, an angler may have to use two-pound test line and troll slowly.

Another strategy that produces slabs when they are in the mouths of creeks is to buoy the schools off and cast to them with either minnows or jigs. However, since these open water schools of crappie are on the move, the fisherman constantly will have to be relocating the schools and moving the buoys -- if he is using this technique. A better method is to utilize his depthfinder and trolling motor to stay on the top of these schools. Then either vertical jig or fish a live minnow straight down to the school to catch the crappie.

MID-WATER CRAPPIE

Most anglers know that before the crappie hit the bank, they usually try and move to some type of mid-water structure that is between the bank and the creek and river channel. For this reason, trolling crappie jigs between the bank and the

A productive place to look for crappie during the pre-spawn is in the mouths of feeder creeks.

edge of the creek channel can be highly productive. The crappie may be holding on little stumps, small brush or sticks that are almost invisible to the depthfinder. But by trolling, an angler can pick up these fish holding in these staging areas. Another advantage of trolling between the creek channel and bank during this time of year is that many times large schools of crappie preparing for the spawn will hold suspended in these regions not relating to any type of cover. But trolling will catch these fish.

SIGHT-FISH CRAPPIE

"I still find crappie the old way," John Hill of Town Creek, Alabama, a nationally known fishing guide on the Tennessee River, reported. "Before and after the spawn, you can locate crappie in shallow water if you know how to sight-fish for them."

Although sight-fishing usually refers to an angler's skill in seeing fish and then catching those fish, when Hill uses the term sight-fish, he is referring to his ability to read what is happening on the surface of the water to determine where the crappie should be.

"When you see diving and feeding coots or ducks along the bank of a point or in a cove before or after the spawn, you know a school of shad is in the area," Hill explained. "Usually crappie will be under or off to the side of the school of baitfish feeding on the same bait the waterfowl are eating."

39

Another tactic Hill utilizes when sight-fishing is to watch for diving gulls. When seagulls spot schools of shad swimming in open water and begin to dive on the baitfish, the shad will move deeper into the water where the crappie are feeding. As the crappie attack the shad and force them to the surface again, the gulls dive on them. The crappie in the water and the gulls above yo-yo a school of shad as both predators feed on the bait.

"Often shad feed along the top of the water with their mouths just out of the water," Hill commented. "Crappie hitting in the school of shad are ones you can catch."

Hill's sight-fishing strategies will help you locate schools of feeding crappie in open water where no one else is fishing in the pre-spawn.

PLANTED CRAPPIE

One of the best ways I know to ensure good catches of pre-spawn crappie is to plant for them. By that I mean sink brush or stake beds halfway between the creek channels and the creek banks. If anglers provide some type of cover for the crappie to hold on when the fish are migrating from the creek channel to the shallow water, the chances are the fishermen will be able to return to that cover within a day or two and take crappie. Sinking cover between the bank and the creek channel not only pays off during the pre-spawn period, but anglers also can catch crappie during the spawn and after the spawn on this same cover.

When crappie start to spawn, they always will be holding on that mid-water cover waiting to go to the bank and waiting to move back into deep water. Even after the spawn, crappie will hold on the brush planted between the creek channel and the bank until the water temperature warms up enough to drive them back to the creek and river channels. Therefore, to make sure you harvest a crop of crappie before, during and just after the spawn, plant cover under the water now.

FLOOD WATER CRAPPIE

"Come on down to my restaurant, John, about 1:00 p.m.," Danny Wiles of Birmingham, Alabama, told me. "I've been fishing, and I've caught a big mess of slab crappie."

Sinking cover between the bank and the creek channel not only pays off during the pre-spawn period, but anglers also can catch crappie during the spawn and after the spawn on this same cover.

I'd always known Wiles was a good fisherman because he consistently caught large crappie and spotted bass in tailrace areas. But until I talked with Wiles on this particular day, I hadn't realized he also was insane.

Our part of the country had had the worst floods in the history of the state for the two days prior to his phone call. The rivers were about to flow out of their banks all over our state, and I knew the spillways below the dams where Wiles fished had to be open and running water. No one in his right mind would have gone fishing the day Wiles went in the wind, rain and muddy water conditions. But at lunchtime when I sat down to drag some tasty, fried, crappie fillets through a puddle of ketchup, I started picking Wiles' brain about how to catch bad weather papermouths.

"I only seriously crappie fish for about three to four weeks during the early spring prior to the spawn," Wiles said. "I've found the best crappie fishing to be on the worst days imaginable for several reasons.

"When the weather's bad, lots of water is coming over the spillways at the dams, the wind's blowing, the current in the river is strong, and the water is muddy, rarely will there be another boat below the dam except mine. Therefore, I don't have any competition for the fish.

"Also, I like to fish on those kinds of days because the current forces the baitfish into eddy holes and pockets downriver behind rocks, below underwater drop-offs and behind trees that have fallen into the river. During these flood water conditions, the baitfish will school up in these eddy holes, and the big crappie will stack up in these same areas while gorging on shad in preparation for the spawn. Usually, I can catch all the crappie I want to take in a half-day's fishing. If I have a limit of 35 fish, I'll generally have five to 10 crappie that will weigh two pounds or more."

Wiles has found one of the best-kept secrets for successful pre-spawn crappie fishing. He fishes at a time and in a place when most other anglers are convinced that fishing will not be productive. However, Wiles has learned that the most productive crappie fishing of the year and when he catches the biggest crappie is when the rivers are flooding, and the weather is too rough for weekend anglers.

A few years ago, I had planned a day off to bank fish for papermouths on a small stream near my home. As luck would have it, the weather turned off foul two days prior to my trip. The rain came down all night long, just before my off-day.

At first light, the sky was still gray and threatening a shower. But I was off from work, I had a bucket of minnows, a rod, a box of hooks and a few shot leads, and I was determined to go fishing. Walking down the bank, I stopped at every point where I saw an eddy hole. All day long, I consistently took crappie in the high water with the fast current. For some reason, those flooding conditions seemed to cause the crappie to go on a feeding spree. All I had to do to catch them was find the slack water areas where the fish could hold out of the current and feed.

But swift current and fast-moving streams are not the only places where anglers can catch high water crappie. When the spring floods come, and many rivers and lakes back up into woodlots and fields, often the crappie will follow the moving water into the newly inundated lands. I fish along a flood plain on the Tennessee/Tombigbee Waterway. Using a flat-bottomed johnboat, I have gone to the river when the water's up and made some large catches in freshly flooded woodlots during the early part of the spring.

One of my favorite places to fish in these conditions is around newly inundated briar thickets where baitfish concentrate. The crappie school up and feed on these baitfish. Also standing timber in very shallow water is another strategic structure to home in on when you're angling for high water papermouths.

The key to catching these shallow water fish is to fish with minnows and jigs and hold the baits only one or two inches under the surface. When the water is muddy and rising, light doesn't penetrate very deeply into the water. Most of the baitfish usually will be swimming in less than a foot of water. The baitfish will be following the moving water into the shallows to feed off the new plant life and microscopic animals that are coming into the lake as the water floods. By keeping your bait in that very shallow water, your minnows or jigs will appear more natural to the crappie, and you'll take more fish.

Most anglers' boats draft too much water or either may be too big to move into these shallow water regions. I prefer to use a small johnboat or a one or two-man type of boat like Coleman's Crawdad or the Bass Hunter, which are easy to maneuver and fish from in backwater areas. Yet another tactic I've used to catch big crappie when the river's up is to carry my Porta-Bote into the woods on my hunting club that's bounded by the river. If I launch the boat in the spring in the woodlots I've hunted in the fall, in many of these regions, which are inaccessible from the river or a road, I have no competition for these flood plain papermouths.

Crappie are members of the sunfish family, which is the same family to which black bass belong. The papermouths will react to rising flood waters just as bass do. They'll be positioned near the edge of the shore in very shallow water, facing toward the bank where the baitfish will be running. The crappie fisherman who understands how and where to find bass when rivers flood also will know where to look for crappie under the same circumstances.

Remember that high water, wind and rain are miserable conditions for anglers. But just as when Brer Fox flung Brer Rabbit into the briarpatch thinking he was putting the cottontail in a terrible place, these are the kinds of conditions on which crappie thrive. Here's where baitfish are more abundant and easy to find since they're holding in the very top story of the water close to the bank or staying out of the current in eddy areas.

For the anglers who are nuts like Danny Wiles and willing to brave the elements, flood water conditions where there's very little fishing pressure from any other anglers can prove to be the best crappie fishing of the year.

- 5 -

HOW TO TAKE SPAWNING CRAPPIE

"This pole will do," John Holley, my fishing buddy in college, told me.

Holley may go down in history as the greatest crappie angler who ever lived. When I fished with Holley, we rarely got skunked. Holley taught me more about crappie fishing than any man I ever have known.

"The butt of the canepole needs to be about the diameter of a pool cue," Holley said. "Next, we'll break off 18 inches of the tip so the pole has plenty of backbone. We'll use 25-pound test monofilament. Then when the hook gets stuck in the brush, we can straighten the hook and not break the line. I like quill corks because they sink easier, and you can see bites better on them than on other kinds of corks. We'll catch our minnows out of the branch because that's cheaper than having to buy them."

We used my aluminum johnboat. Whoever fished in the front of the boat had to do the paddling.

DROP-FISH IN THE THICKEST COVER

From late February through May during crappie spawning season in the Deep South, Holley and I caught some of the finest slab crappie anywhere. Holley's technique was simple. We drop-fished down the bank.

"Most any water has some underwater cover you can't see that crappie can hold on," Holley explained. "Most spring-time crappie fishermen only will fish around visible cover, which means they keep the crappie around this kind of cover caught out most of the time. But by fishing invisible cover, we'll take the big crappie no one else knows are there."

When I was growing up and fished with my dad, he taught me that if someone in the boat caught a fish, the other person should wait and let him pitch his minnow back to that same spot to try and catch another fish. But this was not Holley's philosophy. Before the water came back together when I pulled a crappie out during the spawn, Holley's minnow and cork would be in my spot.

Finally one day I asked, "Aren't you going to let me throw back into the place where I caught that fish?"

With a scowl on his face, Holley looked back and said, "You don't expect me to fish where there aren't any fish, do you? If I catch a crappie out of a spot, I expect you to pitch right back into that place and attempt to catch another crappie while they're biting. Any time we find crappie, we both should try to take as many fish as possible from that spot."

When we found a bush or the top of a tree out in the water, Holley would spend two or three minutes worming his line and cork through the branches to fish the thickest part of the tree.

"All the other anglers are fishing the outside of trees and are catching little crappie," Holley observed. "To catch the big fish, you must put your minnow in the thickest part of the brush during the spawn. Once you get a crappie on, then you can worry about how to get the fish out. If your hook gets hung, straighten the hook out, and keep on fishing. You don't catch big crappie by fishing where everybody else on the lake is angling."

Holley was proven right over and over. Often we would catch 1-1/2- to two-pound crappie in cover so thick I thought we'd have to use a chainsaw to get the fish out of the brush. When we located a site that was producing numbers of crappie, but the fish stopped biting, Holley would leave that spot and go hunt a new place to fish. However, we usually would

By drop-fishing down the bank, you can catch plenty of crappie during the spawn in many areas.

return to that area once or twice during the day and catch even more crappie during the spawn.

ANGLE SMALL CREEKS, STREAMS AND SLOUGHS

"Also, shallow sloughs where no one else fishes at the beginning of spring usually warm up quicker than the main lake or river," Holley mentioned. "Crappie will go to the banks first to spawn in these areas. Since these crappie haven't been harassed by anglers, you generally can catch the biggest and most slabs in these protected waters."

I once fished a small creek that fed into a major reservoir. The water in this creek was somewhat warmer than the water in the lake. Therefore, in the spring when the crappie were looking for warm water areas to spawn in, the fish would move into this creek. No one except my fishing buddy and I knew the papermouths were there.

47

Fishing in thick cover is where you may take the biggest crappie during the spawn.

The creek had a fairly strong flow in it with small peninsulas of land jutting out into the main channel and creating eddies on the downstream sides of the peninsulas. Utilizing 1/32-ounce jigs, small corks and six-pound test line, we cast upstream, allowed our jigs and corks to wash around the peninsulas and into the eddy holes, and caught plenty of slab crappie.

One of the misconceptions associated with fishing for spawning crappie is that anglers primarily must fish from boats to catch fish on major reservoirs. However, I learned early in my fishing career while still in college that anglers could take plenty of slab crappie fishing from the banks in many of the small feeder streams that warmed up first during the spring. I found a small stream less than a mile from my dormitory room. In the spring, anytime I had an hour break between classes, I jumped into my car, drove to the bridge that crossed the stream and took 10 to 15 crappie fishing a jig and cork.

Anglers who fish small streams just prior to and during the spawn often can load their coolers with papermouths and never have to get into a boat. The most productive areas usually are eddy holes behind some type of current break or brush tops or sunken trees and deep holes along the creek. Crappie fishing has become so high-tech that many of us have forgotten how many fish can be taken from the banks by anglers who spend the time walking the banks and hunting crappie holes in the spawn.

USE LIGHT LINE

Another technique that pays crappie dividends in the springtime is fishing light line in thick cover. Most anglers prefer six, eight and even 10-pound test line for fishing shoreline cover for crappie. However, through experimentation, I have found I get more strikes and catch more crappie when I fish two or four-pound test Trilene XT line. Lighter line does not spook crappie as much and also allows minnows to have more action. By using a limber fiberglass pole like B & M's Buck's Classic and not being impatient, I slowly and carefully can work the crappie out of cover and bring them to the boat without breaking my line.

FISH THE MOST SHALLOW PLACES

The strangest crappie tactic during the spawn I ever had seen was when I watched a pole fisherman fish down a bank which had a large amount of fallen timber in the shallow water. This angler, who had his round cork attached to the line right at the eye of the hook, would swing the bobber and the minnow into the water, which often was less than six inches deep. He consistently caught more crappie than I did.

When I questioned him about his fishing techniques, he explained that, "I've found that during the spawn, crappie often are in much more shallow water than most people think. I've even seen crappie spawning with their backs out of the water. Remember that shallow water is where baitfish also will be. By fishing in ankle-deep water, I can catch big crappie that most other anglers never believe will be in water that shallow."

And the man's stringer of crappie proved his success.

Even small anglers can catch big crappie from the bank in the spawn.

Another time during spring crappie spawning season as I sat on the edge of a backwater slough dressed in full camouflage, called to turkeys and waited on a longbeard to show up, I heard a hen cackle. When my gobbler became silent, I felt sure he had gone to her.

Disappointed, I remained on my stand and watched two anglers drop fishing along the edge of the timber-infested slough in water not more than two or three feet deep. These anglers consistently pulled double-hand-sized crappie from around the logs and limbs right up against the bank.

Silently slipping my hand into my hunting vest, I retrieved my binoculars to spy on the unsuspecting fishermen. Their round red and white corks were set only three inches up their lines from the minnows they dropped into only four or five inches of water. I was surprised crappie could swim in water so shallow. Turkeys forgotten, I walked down the bank to the two surprised anglers and asked how they were catching crappie in that very shallow water.

The angler in the stern of the boat replied, "We always catch the biggest crappie of the year -- usually the first spawning crappie -- in water less than a foot deep. Shallow water heats up faster than deep water after the winter. When the crappie move in to spawn, they're looking for minnows and baitfish right along the bank."

The man in the bow of the boat explained that, "If you'll watch the bank when the water begins to warm, you'll find baitfish next to the bank. We start fishing about a week or two before anyone else does, and we generally catch the first big spawning crappie that move to the bank to feed."

These anglers fished virgin water no other crappiers fished -- very shallow and close to the bank. Each year, they told me, they always caught numbers of large crappie.

FISH A COLD FRONT

One of the worse things that can happen when crappie go to the bank to spawn is for a cold front to hit. To be successful, you must learn how to locate crappie then. If crappie have been spawning in a particular bay or slough, then when the cold front comes through, they usually will not leave that area. However, instead of being on the bank, they most often will move to the middle of the slough. If you are minnow or jig fishing, fish a little deeper, and move further away from the bank.

Jimmy Dixon, a friend of mine, put it best when he said, "My favorite time to fish during the spawn is the day a cold front hits and the following three or four days. During those times, all the other crappie fishermen either will leave the lake or else cannot find fish. But I know the crappie must be on the first bottom break away from the shore or on secondary creek channels or drop-offs close to the spawning areas. Because the crappie almost always are schooled-up, I can take more crappie in a shorter time than I can on those warmer and prettier days when everyone else is fishing for crappie."

ANGLE DEEP WATER STRUCTURES

Most anglers hit the banks for papermouths during the spawn. The fish, which are moving into shallow water, generally are found close to any type of cover along the bank. However, Dr. Tom Forsyth, a fisheries biologist for the Tennessee Valley Authority (TVA) reported that, "Not all female crappie go to the bank at the same time to spawn, nor do they spawn one time and then leave the bank. The females may move to the bank two to four times before they spawn out all their eggs. When they do go to the bank, they rarely stay more than an hour or two before they retreat to deeper water to wait to spawn again. To more consistently catch the larger female spawners, anglers should fish the deeper water structures."

The deeper water structures Forsyth is referring to are the small ditches, cuts and cover on the edges of the shallow water breaklines and/or brush shelters built on points that provide cover for the crappie while they're waiting to spawn. The largest number of fish actually on the bank in the spring will be the male crappie that are roaming the bank, fertilizing the eggs that are deposited by the females.

Forsyth's information was proven last spring when I fished with Philip Criss and Cary Arnold of Alabama, both avid bass anglers. Arnold and Criss reluctantly had agreed to fish for crappie because there were some one-pound to two-pound papermouths in two feet of water along the edges of the pepper grass.

As Criss and I dropped minnows on canepoles next to the grass and caught heavy speckled-sides, Arnold cast a small Beetle Spin on four pound test line out in the middle of the slough because he refused to use any tactic that might simulate crappie fishing. However, Arnold consistently caught more and bigger crappie in the middle of the slough around no apparent cover than Criss and I took fishing the edges of the weeds. Apparently, the largest number of big spawners were holding in the middle of the slough in the deeper water waiting their turns to come to the bank and spawn.

Fishing very deep water during the spawn can produce large stringers of nice-sized crappie.

Ruby Hughley and Reba Yurgin are crappie fishing guides on Kentucky Lake in Tennessee who also have proven that often the bigger sized crappie will be holding in deeper water just off the bank throughout much of the spawn.

"A few years ago Ruby and I found this little secondary creek channel that dropped off from three feet to five feet about 40 yards from a spawning flat," Yurgin said. "Although this small creek channel was so insignificant that most other anglers wouldn't fish it, the creek had some underwater stumps on the edge of the old creekbank that we located with our depthfinder. By trolling this little ditch with three to six poles with three to four feet of line on each and 1/24- or 1/32-ounce jigs, we regularly caught more and larger crappie than the people who were fishing visible cover next to the bank -- even during the spawn. We used our trolling motor to slowly move the boat along the edge of that break."

Joe Wilson of Columbus, Mississippi, fishes for crappie in even deeper water during the spring months because he has found that, "Crappie live on river and creek channels their entire lives. Oftentimes they will vacation in shallow water or move into shallow water to spawn, but the deep water is their home."

To locate the bottom breaks and the cover on these breaks, Wilson uses a Humminbird LCR depthfinder. He fishes with an eight-foot Buck's Classic graphite crappie pole and minnows.

"I prefer using a shorter pole like the Buck's Classic because I can fish directly under the transducer of my depthfinder that's mounted to the foot of my trolling motor," Wilson mentioned. "Using this technique means I can see the cover I'm fishing while I'm fishing it -- even though the cover is submerged. I like the soft tip of this crappie pole, which bends and gives the minnow to the crappie better than even an ultralight rod will. Yet I have the power in the middle and the butt of the pole to break the crappie away from the cover and be able to pull the fish all the way into the boat. By fishing the creek and river channels, I catch more and bigger crappie year-round.

"One of the problems associated with spring crappie fishing is finding the papermouths when a cold front hits, or when the water temperature warms up, and the spawn is over. These are the times when crappie leave the shallows. However, by fishing the river and creek channels, I can catch all the crappie I want -- no matter what the weather conditions are."

MAKE SET-OUTS

Another strategy deadly for spawning crappie is one I learned from Red Cotton, a 75-year-old angler from West Point, Mississippi, who makes set-outs. Cotton's set-outs are much like a duck hunter's decoy spread. Cotton utilizes beaver sticks to lure in and hold passing crappie until he can catch them.

As Cotton explained to me, "I stick beaver sticks, which are poles from four to six feet long that beavers have gnawed all of the bark off, in the mud in the bottoms of shallow coves with little or no cover where crappie normally spawn -- usually about 15 yards away from a bank. I set out the poles 10 to 12 yards apart so the tips are visible above the water. Just prior to the spawn, during the spawn and after the spawn,

Not all female crappie go to the bank at the same time to spawn, nor do they spawn one time and then leave the bank.

I average one to two crappie around each beaver stick in a day of fishing with a fiberglass pole and a jig.

"Crappie will associate with a beaver stick and protect that stick from other crappie. These fish generally are the bigger crappie. Maybe the bigger crappie run the smaller crappie away from the sticks. Since the stick provides an ambush point for the crappie, when the crappie see a small jig swimming by the stick, the fish will attack the jig."

Cotton uses a B & M graphite pole with four feet of eight-pound test line and a 1/32-ounce jig. By twitching the end of the pole, Cotton makes the jig hop as he utilizes the pole to swim the bait around and up and down the set-outs.

An advantage to fishing set-outs is that most other anglers will not fish them because they appear to be such sparse cover that many sportsmen think they will not hold crappie. But when I fished with Cotton, I learned that although the beaver sticks did not hold the numbers of crappie other spots might, the one or two crappie we caught around each stick almost always were the bigger crappie. To catch more crappie, an angler merely makes more set-outs.

There is no trick to catching springtime crappie when the fish are on the banks. Generally they feed very heavily, bite readily and are easy to take. If you want to catch crappie this spawning season, fish the way you always have. To take very big crappie and plenty of them, find the out-of-the-way places where no one else is fishing, and utilize some of these methods for catching spawning crappie.

- 6 -

HOW TO CATCH POST-SPAWN CRAPPIE

An angler who can answer the questions of when the post-spawn is, what a post-spawn crappie is, and how a fisherman catches crappie when they are not on the banks can extend his crappie season each year -- often by as much as a month.

Most papermouth anglers assume that prime crappie season is the time during the spring when the slabs move into the shallow water to spawn. While the crappie are on the banks, they are relatively easy to catch with almost any type of tackle by fishermen with even just a small amount of angling experience. But when the spring run is over, most anglers have a difficult time taking papermouths.

What many anglers do not understand is that all crappie do not go to the banks at the same time -- even during the spring run. Here's what the experts say about the post-spawn.

DR. TOM FORSYTH - FISHERIES SCIENTIST

According to Dr. Tom Forsyth, Coordinator of Research Development at Land Between the Lakes in Kentucky for the Tennessee Valley Authority (TVA), whose Ph.D. is in fisheries, "Generally when the female crappie go to the bank to spawn, they only may remain on the bank for an hour or two, spawning out perhaps 20 percent of their eggs. Then these females move out into the deeper water while the males that are constantly on the bank fertilize the females' eggs.

"During the spawn, one female may return to the bank three or four times until she is spawned out. Different males fertilize her eggs, which is why crappie do not have an inbreeding problem. Therefore, even at the peak of the spawn, as many males and females will be in the deeper water waiting to spawn as are in the shallow water spawning.

"My experience has been that after the spawn is over, the crappie tend to move away from the shoreline and scatter out more. On Kentucky Lake and other lakes with which I'm the most familiar, the crappie spawn usually occurs in some types of embayment. After the spawn, the scattered crappie seem to be more in the middle of the embayment than along the edges. To catch post-spawn crappie, anglers who are drift-fishing live bait or trolling jigs may catch as many, if not more, crappie than the anglers who are fishing sunken brush and ledges and other bottom drop-offs."

With the crappie scattered over a much greater area immediately after the spawn, the more water you can cover trolling, the more crappie you can catch. Also, because crappie will be holding between the creek channel and the bank, anglers who are accomplished in the art of trolling can move their boats up and down the water between the bank and the creek channel, cover a large region, and often take many fish.

Drift fishing with either minnows or jigs at this time of year is also extremely productive. Dr. Forsyth's theory that crappie stay in the embayments right after the spawn means that, even though there may not be a creek or river channel close to a spawning flat, anglers are more likely to catch crappie trolling and drift fishing in the middle of the sloughs and bays than they are leaving the sloughs and bays and moving to the creek channels.

The fact that post-spawn crappie are primarily rovers is good news and bad news. The good news is that if you catch a good number of crappie on a drop-off, ledge or brush, and if the fish stop biting, a new group of crappie may move into that same cover within an hour or two or on the next day. The bad news is that you may locate a good bunch of crappie on a spot one day and return the next day yet not get a bite.

Trolling is an effective method for catching crappie immediately after the spawn.

SAM HEATON - CRAPPIE GUIDE

A man who makes his living as a crappie guide on Weiss Lake on the northern Alabama/Georgia border is Sam Heaton of Centre, Alabama, who works out of Bay Springs Marina. Every year Heaton is faced with the problem of catching post-spawn crappie.

"Post-spawn crappie aren't as hard to catch as many people will have you believe," Heaton says. "You find the post-spawn crappie at the same places where you locate pre-spawn crappie. They usually will be holding on the ledges and drop-offs close to the shallow water where they've spawned before they return to deep water.

"On Weiss Lake, I generally discover most post-spawn crappie in about 10 or 15 feet of water. Usually I'll be catching crappie on brush piles that have been put into the lake just to concentrate post-spawn and pre-spawn crappie. At Weiss, numbers of folks cut down trees along the banks to provide spots where crappie can hold. But I've found that

59

Sam Heaton of Gadsden, Alabama, finds plenty of post-spawn crappie in brush piles in 12 to 15 feet of water close to spawning areas.

brush piles further out in the water are far more productive and allow me to lengthen my season by at least a month prior to, and a month after, the spawn.

"Brush piles in 12 to 15 feet of water close to spawning areas will be utilized by crappie during the pre-spawn period to hold on to wait for the correct water temperature to go to the banks and spawn. During the post-spawn time, the crappie coming away from the bank will concentrate on these same brush piles and feed on shad to build their body weights back up and to wait for the warmer weather that will drive them back to the deeper creek channels. These brush piles generally will home crappie until the surface temperature of the water reaches about 85 to 86 degrees.

"During this time of year, most of the time I locate crappie in water where the pH is between 7-1/2 and 8-1/2 and with a water temperature of less than 70 degrees. The best places to build these brush piles is where two creek channels come together, an underwater point, or where there's a cut-back in an old creek or river channel. If you don't want to build brush piles, look for natural cover like old stumprows or sunken trees in these areas.

"My favorite technique for catching these crappie is to use a standard crappie rig with a lead weight on the bottom and two drop-lines coming off the main line. Then bait with minnows and bump the crappie rigs in the brush.

"Two tricks are involved in taking crappie with this technique -- using a light wire hook like an 860 Tru-Turn light wire or a No. 2 Eagle Claw hook and fishing with 12- to 17-pound test line. Utilize the heavier line, which lets you pull on the line and straighten the hooks out without tearing up too much of the cover when you get hung. Also, remember to stay straight above the brush you're fishing. Don't drag your line through the brush, or else you'll stay hung and won't catch many crappie."

CHARLIE INGRAM - CRAPPIE GUIDE

Charlie Ingram from Tom Mann's Fish World Guide Service in Eufaula, Alabama, guides crappie anglers on Lake Eufaula on the Georgia/Alabama border.

"I've found that brush piles on points that lead into shallow bays and coves are the most productive for taking crappie prior to, during and after the crappie spawn," Ingram mentions. "The brush piles I fish are in eight to 12 feet of water. I've learned that crappie will gang up on this brush before they go in to spawn. Even during the spawn while everybody else is fishing next to the bank, I'm still taking plenty of big crappie out on these brush piles. Also, I've noticed the crappie I'm catching are bigger crappie than what the bank-bound anglers are taking.

"After the crappie have left the banks, my fish are still holding on those brush piles. I usually can continue to catch crappie until the water heats up so much it forces the crappie into deeper water. Oftentimes, even during the summer months, on the brush that's close to the river ledges, I'll take crappie moving up into this brush early in the morning and late in the afternoon. I believe that providing that brush away from the bank in eight to 12 feet of water allows me to consistently catch crappie throughout most of the year.

"How I catch the crappie out of the brush depends on the water clarity at the time I fish. If the water is stained, then I can move right over the brush and fish down in the cover,

Laurie Lee Dovey of Alpharetta, Georgia, catches post-spawn slabs for the skillet from brush piled in front of docks and piers.

using a 3/4-ounce jigging spoon. By slowly lowering and raising my rod tip, I can get the crappie to take the big spoon. The line size doesn't seem to matter. But in clear water, I back away from the cover and cast to it, using 1/24-ounce jigs and six-pound test line."

ROGER JARVIS - NATIONAL CRAPPIETHON CHAMPION

Roger Jarvis of Nashville, Tennessee, one of the 1987 Crappiethon Classic winners, agrees with Heaton and Ingram about where to search for post-spawn crappie.

"I look for the first small drop away from the bank, between the spawning area and the creek channels, on which the crappie can hold. Although the bottom may drop two or three times before it slopes off into the creek channel, post-spawn crappie usually will concentrate on that very first drop on whatever cover is available on that bottom break.

Charlie Ingram shows young John Phillips, Jr. how to take crappie from brush piles on points.

"To catch these crappie, my fishing partner, Sterling Earhart, and I will be pitching jigs to these ledges and drop-offs and vertical jigging down through the structure. Water clarity dictates which method of fishing we'll use. If the water is extremely clear, then we'll back away from the structure and pitch to it. But if the water is stained, we'll vertical jig right on top of the structure."

There are secret holes that anglers who fish for post-spawn crappie know are almost sure-fire. One of these spots is the brush that usually is piled in front of boatdocks and piers on lakes and rivers by lakeside residences. These regions generally will hold crappie during post-spawn periods because they provide cover at depths which the fish want to hold, and they are close to the bank. Other sites that pay crappie dividends are bridge pilings, railroad trestles and any other kind of vertical structure that the crappie can relate to that is relatively close to the bank and will hold baitfish.

The two factors that seem to cause post-spawn crappie to school tighter and in larger numbers are water temperature and the amount of dissolved oxygen in the water. As the weather heats up, crappie will dive deeper to find the cooler water. But as the summer comes, water gives up a lot of oxygen due to the heat. Therefore, the crappie have to be compressed into tighter schools because there is less water in the lake at their temperature comfort zone and with enough dissolved oxygen to sustain life.

If you are fishing during the first part of the post-spawn when the crappie have just come off the bank, the fish will tend to be more scattered than later during the post-spawn when the water temperature warms up and the oxygen level in the lake decreases.

Another limiting factor that helps determine how quickly the crappie school up after the spawn is the amount of flow coming through a reservoir. If the spring season is relatively dry as is the early summer, and the flow in the lakes and rivers is reduced, then the crappie will bunch up quicker after the spawn than if a good flow of water comes through the lake throughout the spring and summer. Too, the flow often determines the amount of oxygen content in the lake. Areas of less oxygen will hold fewer crappie.

If you read many articles about crappie and crappie fishing, you will realize that the recent emphasis has been on fishing for pre-spawn crappie. More and more anglers are learning how to find the papermouths just before they go to the bank. But what many fishermen fail to realize is that right after the spawn, there often will be plenty of crappie in the same places where they found pre-spawn crappie.

- 7 -

HOW TO TAKE SUMMERTIME CRAPPIE

During the spring spawn in many lakes, a person can just about walk from boat to boat as anglers attack the shoreline harvesting the rich bounty of crappie that move into shallow water to lay their eggs. But when the spawn is over, and the crappie leave the shallows, so do the fishermen. Although still plenty of crappie are in a lake to be caught, many anglers do not know where to find the crappie or how to catch them.

"Ninety-five percent of the anglers who fish for crappie angle only the visible cover along the shore that they can see," Ken Cook of Meers, Oklahoma, says. "However, the crappie are only in that shallow water cover for approximately two months of the year. The rest of the time, they usually are holding in deep water along some type of bottom break structure and near or in some type of cover. If you want to take crappie in the summertime, you must learn how to use your depthfinder and locate the fish in open water because that's what summertime crappie fishing is all about."

Often when bass fishing is slow in the summer, and the bass angler gets those little pecks on his line, he can convert over to crappie fishing and catch a good mess of slabs even if the bass will not hit. Then the angler can take the crappie home to eat and still catch and release the bass.

Ken Cook, who is not only the winner of the 1991 B.A.S.S. Masters Classic and a Megabucks tournament but also is a fisheries biologist whose knowledge of fish and angling encompasses more than the sport of tournament bass fishing, says, "Fishermen can eat crappie because crappie are such a prolific fish. In most lakes across the country, there are healthy crappie populations that can be harvested heavily each year without impacting the resource because crappie can withstand much more fishing pressure than bass. In many areas of the country, crappie are so overpopulated that the fish's growth becomes stunted.

"However, to prevent overharvesting of crappie, abide by the rules and regulations set by the fisheries departments in each state. State fisheries biologists know what they're doing, and set seasons and bag limits for crappie on particular lakes to allow maximum harvest without impacting the resource."

Cook believes that crappie fishing in the middle of the day during the summertime can provide an excellent break for the bass angler who knows that mid-day fishing for largemouths can be tough.

"I've never met a fish I didn't like, and crappie not only provide a fun tug on the line in the middle of the day, but they're an excellent eating fish and a good freezer stocker," Cook explains. "Although bass seem to be most active early and late during the hot summer months, crappie may feed three or four times a day and usually are more likely to be active in the middle of the day than the bass. There's no reason why the bass fisherman can't return home with a mess of fish to eat -- if he uses his bass tactics to catch crappie when the bass aren't biting."

According to Cook, "Remembering that the crappie is a member of the sunfish family just like the bass is important because these two species are similar in many ways. They're both very structure- and cover-oriented, and both fish during the spawn fan a bed in fairly shallow water and deposit their eggs, which is the time when both crappie and bass are easier to take. After the spawn, both bass and crappie move to deep water, which is when most anglers have a difficult time catching crappie or bass."

As a fisheries biologist and avid angler, 1991 B.A.S.S. Masters Classic Champion, Ken Cook of Meers, Oklahoma, has numerous tips for catching summertime crappie.

When crappie come off the bank to move to deep water, they often become edge feeders -- swimming and holding along various edges like ledges and drop-offs.

FIND THE PH BREAKLINE AND THERMOCLINE

As Cook explains, "The drop-offs along major creek and river channels often are the best places to locate crappie during the summer months. I find crappie in the summer in the same way I do bass, which involves three steps.

Once you find the pH and the thermocline breaklines in the water in the summer, you often will discover crappie.

"During the summer, and especially the hottest summer months, anglers know that crappie are hunting a water temperature that is comfortable to them that has plenty of dissolved oxygen. The first step is to determine where the pH breakline and thermocline are. The pH breakline will show us where the ideal pH is, and the thermocline will denote where the ideal water temperature is. Usually, the pH breakline will sit right on top of the thermocline. To find these breaklines, I use a pH meter and find at what depth I get a pH and a temperature breakline.

"There's another method of finding this breakline where not only crappie and bass but just about all the fish in a lake hold on and that's by running your boat across the lake and taking note at what depth you spot fish showing up on your depthfinder. By averaging the depths where you see the most fish, you reasonably can assume that this is the thermocline and pH breakline."

LOCATE A BOTTOM BREAK

"The second step to finding crappie in the hot summer months is to locate a bottom break, which creates an edge that the crappie will travel along, that intersects the water

68

depth where the proper pH and thermocline are," Cook says. "With these two factors, we know the water depth the crappie will be the most comfortable in and have found the ledge where they want to feed."

PINPOINT COVER

"The only thing lacking is the third ingredient --cover, which I define as some kind of brush, stumps, logs or anything that the crappie can lie next to, get under, or get inside of," Cook mentions. "I use these three ingredients like a road map. I locate the water temperature and thermocline the crappie prefer first. Then I follow that water temperature line until I intersect structure. Then I follow that structure until I discover cover. This is a simple, basic formula for locating crappie on any lake the same way bass anglers find bass in the summertime."

FISH WITH LIGHT TACKLE

"One of the biggest differences in finding and catching crappie and locating and taking bass during the summer months is the crappie fisherman uses smaller baits and lighter tackle," Cook reports. An advantage to finding crappie in the summer months is that they tend to school up tighter than bass do. When you catch one crappie, you usually can assume there are more crappie in the area. Generally I fish around the spot where I've taken that first fish and anticipate catching a lot more crappie."

USE A DEPTHFINDER

Probably the number one tool of the summertime crappie angler is the depthfinder, which shows an angler the bottom breaks that he can follow until he sees the cover and locates schools of crappie holding over the cover. However, depthfinders may be as much a a hindrance as a help in finding crappie. Some anglers will not fish a piece of cover if the depthfinder does not show crappie holding on that cover. But during the summer months, crappie may be holding in and under cover and will not show up on a depthfinder. The angler who does not stop to fish that cover may be missing an opportunity to take papermouths home to the skillet.

This is why many anglers like Ken Cook fish cover -- whether they see fish or not -- because as Cook comments, "Crappie tend to school at a particular depth according to water temperature and dissolved oxygen content. Many times if the crappie aren't in the cover, they'll be schooled up above or under the cover or off to the side of it."

According to Dr. Tom Forsyth, who has a Ph.D. in fisheries, "When you discover a school of fish like this in the summer, you can assume several things about them:

* "Vertical jigging or fishing deep with minnows right on top of the schools will be the best method to catch these crappie. They will leave the cover to take the bait.

* "You can return to that same school for several days without the school's having moved. What actually happens in the summertime is the amount of water the crappie can survive in shrinks drastically. Therefore, the crappie have to be concentrated in larger schools to survive. To locate crappie, an angler must utilize a depthfinder. However, he'll have to look in much less water for the fish than he did during the post-spawn time of the year when the water conditions were better for the crappie.

"The advantage to summertime fishing for crappie is that if an angler can fish consecutively for three or four days, he can go to the same place where he has located the schools and continue to catch fish in those schools all three days. If an angler learns how to take crappie in the summer, he consistently can catch more fish than he will during the spring when the crappie go to the banks, because the crappie are more concentrated in the summer than they are in springtime."

TALK TO BASS FISHERMEN

Another key to finding crappie in the hot summer months is using the bass fisherman for a birddog. Many times when bass anglers are fishing points, ledges, drop-offs, deep cover and structure, they will have numbers of small pecks on their plastic worms or crankbaits but will not catch the fish. More than likely these strikes are either crappie or bluegills.

Roger Jarvis of Nashville, Tennessee, believes that oftentimes the make-up of the lake itself dictates where you will find the crappie.

I believe crappie must have large egos because often they will try to kill and eat a bait that is too big for them to swallow. So a crappie will attack the larger lures being fished by bass anglers. Therefore, talk to bass fishermen, and ask about places where they have had numbers of light bites. Then go to that same area with your light line and crappie lures or live minnows, and you easily may come home, with a limit of crappie.

DETERMINE THE BEST BAIT

Once you have found the crappie in the summer, you next must determine how to catch them. Using small jigs from 1/16- to 1/32-ounce is Cook's favorite tactic.

71

"I like four to six pound Trimax line, and I fish the little jigs on a slow, steady retrieve," Cook reports. "Crappie, unlike bass, don't like a hopping or a jerking type of retrieve but rather prefer a slower, easier to catch bait. Of course, in hot weather, crappie may be ornery about hitting any bait. If I can see the fish but can't catch them, I'll try Fish Formula's SparklScales on my jigs, which is a product that puts scent in the water as well as gives off a flash that attracts the crappie's attention. If this doesn't work, the bait of last resort is the live minnow. Even a crappie that doesn't want to feed and isn't hungry just has to hit a live minnow swimming in front of its nose."

SET THE HOOK PROPERLY

"Setting the hook correctly is important, too, in catching crappie," Cook advises. "Crappie are like bass. They inhale the bait. As soon as you feel the slightest twitch on the line, set the hook. However, since crappie have tender mouths, don't set the hook too hard, or you'll lose the fish. Most of the time when you feel the bite, the crappie already has taken the bait."

FISH BRIDGE PILINGS AND RAILROAD TRESTLES

"Another area that provides cover in deep water along creek channels and river ledges is bridge pilings and railroad trestles that cross major creek and river channels," Cook says. "During the hot summer months, these vertical structures that go from the bottom to above the surface allow a crappie to hold in any depth of water in which it wants to hold. Plus, if there is current coming through the lake, the bridge pilings offer a current break where baitfish and crappie can hold. Fishing bridge pilings either by day or night can pay major crappie dividends for the summertime crappie angler."

UTILIZE BUOYS

"Yet another tactic that anglers can use once they understand the three steps to finding crappie is what I call the buoy technique," Cook explains. "Once you locate the proper water depth with the right temperature and right amount of

Many times, crappie will be schooled up above or under the cover or off to the side of it.

oxygen content that intersects a creek or a river channel, you can buoy off 200 to 300 yards of the edge of the old creek channel and then motor your boat between your buoys. Although crappie prefer to hold on cover, large schools of crappie will travel up and down these edges, feeding, swimming together, and moving from location to location. When you see a school of fish on your depthfinder between the buoys you have out, drop another buoy to mark the school. Before, I have found as many as three different schools of crappie within 100 yards along the edge of an old creek channel.

"Then go back and fish for the crappie in each school that you have marked. When one school quits biting, move to the next buoy and fish for another school. After you have fished all the schools you have marked, and the fish have stopped biting, you can pick up your buoys, run the same 100 yards of underwater creekbank, often relocate the schools, rebuoy them off and continue to fish. Or, mark another 100 yards of underwater creekbank, and repeat the same procedure. By marking the edges, looking for the fish and buoying off the fish, anglers often can take large numbers of crappie all day long along the edge of one creek channel in the summer."

Bobby Martin of Warner Robins, Georgia, is one of the nation's top crappie fishermen because he knows where and how to find crappie even in the hottest summer months.

DETERMINE THE TYPE OF LAKE YOU'RE FISHING

Roger Jarvis of Nashville, Tennessee, with his partner, Sterling Earhart, won the 1987 Crappiethon Classic. Jarvis is a professional crappie fisherman who knows the ways of summertime crappie.

"I've found that the type of lake more than any other factor dictates where you'll find crappie and how you'll catch them during the summer months," Jarvis reports. "Let's look at some different lakes and how best to catch crappie on them in the summertime.

"On Percy Priest in Tennessee, the oxygen content is the key factor in whether or not crappie bite. Since there's not a lot of flow coming through the lake, the right oxygen content level is critical to finding crappie at Percy Priest. I've seen crappie hold in 80 degree water at Percy Priest to find the best pH. To locate the correct oxygen level, find the pH breakline.

"For instance, if I'm lowering my pH meter into the water and the pH continues to remain the same, at the depth where

74

Little jigs like a 1/32-ounce can produce big crappie during the hot summer months.

there's a two to three degree difference in pH is what I consider a pH breakline. That depth also is usually where the crappie will concentrate on structure.

"Since Weiss Lake in Alabama is built in the confluence of three rivers, there's generally plenty of oxygen in the lake due to the great amount of flow. At Weiss, finding the crappie's preferred water temperature is the critical factor in whether or not an angler catches summertime crappie there. If the surface temperature of Weiss is 80 degrees, then Sterling and I will be looking for water with temperatures in the mid to low 70's at a water depth where the sunlight is not penetrating too deeply. Also we're searching for structure that will hold crappie.

"Because Weiss Lake is usually stained, the primary factor for finding crappie there in the summer are learning where the cover is that the fish prefer that intersects cooler water. In other words, we're looking for where the thermocline crosses cover that allows the fish to dodge the sunlight.

"Lake Hamilton in Hot Springs, Arkansas, is a crystal-clear, spring-fed lake. On this lake, the depth to which sunlight penetrates in the summer is one of the critical elements for locating crappie. Because the lake is spring-fed, the water temperature and the dissolved oxygen content are not as important ingredients on Lake Hamilton for catching crappie as at some other lakes. But, because the lake is so crystal-clear, the crappie are hunting shade during the summer months.

"One of the problems we encountered at Lake Hamilton in past years was that once we found ledges and drop-offs in the depth of water that protected crappie from the sun, this water was too cold for the fish to be comfortable. Most of the water in this lake that was deep enough for the crappie to hide from the sun registered 62 to 63 degrees. Sterling and I had to search until we located ledges and drop-offs with brush on them that were deep enough for the crappie to avoid the sun but that were warmer than the 62-degree water present in similar areas of the lake.

"Finally we discovered some 68-degree water on a drop-off with brush on it where the surface temperature was 76 and 78 degrees. What we had to do on this particular lake was attempt to find the warmer water that was deep enough for the crappie to dodge the sun when the water below this level was too cold for the crappie's comfort zone. Usually, these regions were in 12 to 18 feet of water in the summer."

FISH DEEP WITH TINY JIGS

Bobby Martin of Warner Robbins, Georgia, and his partner, Alan Padgett, who won the 1986 Crappiethon Classic, today are two of the nation's top crappie fishing pros. These two anglers crappie fish more than 200 days per year and fish both the Crappiethon and U.S. Crappie tournament trails.

"The way to catch crappie in the summer is to fish deep," Martin says. "That means most of the time, crappie fishermen can forget about trolling during the summer months. However, there are no hard, fast rules in fishing that don't have an exception. I must explain that you always fish deep in the summer -- unless you encounter some kind of water condition that prevents you from fishing as deeply as normal.

"There's a place on Lake Eufaula in Alabama where three creek channels come together, which is about the only place I know of in the nation, even in August, where an angler always can catch crappie. Crappie concentrate in this particular region because there's cool water from three different creeks running into the lake at the same spot. There will be from 10 to 15 degrees difference in the water temperature in the summer between this area and anywhere else on the lake. Although the rest of Lake Eufaula may have 85 to 90 degree water, the water here constantly will be 65 to 70 degrees from the surface down to about six feet. The fish will be 4-1/2- to 5 feet deep -- even in August.

"This site also has humps on the bottom with trash piled on top of the humps. The crappie have cool water, structure and cover all in one place. Since the water here is always stained, the light penetration doesn't bother the fish either. Because the water temperature in this area remains constant, you can catch crappie trolling all year long on this one area of Lake Eufaula.

"Another effective technique is to vertical jig drop-offs in deep water, much like a bass angler when he's trying to catch bass at this time of the year. Actually, bass angling and crappie fishing are not that much different. Usually, you can find both kinds of fish holding on the same type of structure at the same water depth at about the same time of the year.

"During this hot weather, you'll be fishing a 1/32-ounce jig on four to six pound test line, since crappie seem to want a smaller jig when they're holding in deep water. Of course, when you're fishing a 1/32-ounce jig in water over 12 feet deep, you have plenty of time to talk to your buddy before your jig reaches the bottom. But also, you'd better be watching your line because you'll see the bite rather than feel it.

"Usually crappie are more aggressive when you're fishing light line and little jigs in deep water. Perhaps that's because the baits that are so small and are passing right in front of their noses, which means they don't have to move to hit the lures. So the crappie will suck the jigs in quickly."

SHOOT BOATDOCKS AND PIERS

"Another place where you can find crappie during the hot summer months or for that matter at any time of the year is under boatdocks and piers," Martin explains. "Probably 90 percent of the time, these docks, which will be in fairly deep

77

water, will have brush under them. These docks will home baitfish, and the crappie will follow the baitfish to these spots.

"To fish these boatdocks and piers, I hold a 1/32-ounce jig between my thumb and index finger with the hook pointing out. Then using an ultralight spinning rod and keeping my line tight, I pull the jig back so the rod bows and then releases the jig and the line, which makes the rod shoot the jig up under the low docks. This method allows my fishing partner, Alan Padgett, and myself to get our baits under docks where we normally couldn't cast. Then we can catch the crappie holding on those sites. But most of the time to catch crappie in the summer, you must look for docks that are sitting in eight to 10 feet of water."

- 8 -

WHY FISH BLACK NIGHTS IN HOT WEATHER FOR CRAPPIE

The night was muggy. The big, thick, mushroom-shaped clouds allowed the moon only an occasional glimpse of our boat out in the middle of Lake Martin near my home. Large swarms of gnats, mosquitos and sometimes a mayfly, circled the white beam from the Coleman lantern being cast into the dark water below. Often the heat from the lantern toasted the wings of the bugs, which were inhaled by swarms of shad as soon as they hit the surface of the water. We'd been fishing for three hours and only caught two or three small crappie.

"Sometimes the papermouths don't turn on until 1:00 or 2:00 a.m. in the morning," Randy Sharman, a fishing buddy of mine, explained. "But if and when the crappie start biting, we'll take plenty of good-sized crappie. The fishing will be so fast and furious you can catch two crappie at a time."

At 2:48:30 a.m., large numbers of slab-sized crappie began to school up under the light. We caught the fish from two feet off the bottom to two inches from the surface in the 15-foot deep water. Until the sun came up, the fishing was non-stop. I held the record for the most crappie caught on one minnow when I put my fifth fish in the boat and finally retired the bait. Four of us kept 150 crappie that weighed between 1/2 and 2-1/2 pounds each. On most good crappie lakes, trips like this will occur frequently throughout the summer months.

Night fishing for crappie during the summer often can be more productive than during the spring spawn. Pictured are Randy Sharman, left, and Gaines Hodnett, right.

WHAT EQUIPMENT IS NEEDED
FOR STARLIGHT CRAPPIE

"The biggest problem with fishing for crappie during the hot summer months is keeping your minnows alive and lively," Sharman had mentioned to me before we fished for crappie. "Because the water is so hot, an aerator is a must."

I like an aerator like B & M's Max-Air since it puts out millions of bubbles that come from the bottom of my bucket and float to the surface. But aeration alone will not keep minnows from dying.

80

According to Gaines Hodnett, another angling friend of mine, "Fill plastic medicine bottles 3/4 of the way to the top with water. Then screw the lids tight on the bottles, and put the bottles in the freezer. As soon as you buy your minnows from the bait store, place one of these bottles of frozen water in your minnow bucket.

"I used to put ice straight in my minnow water, but apparently some of the minerals in the ice killed the minnows. Since I've started utilizing the iced medicine bottles and the aerator, I rarely lose a bait."

For a rod, I like either a lightweight B & M crappie rod, a Zebco ultralight rod or one of Berkley's new graphite ultralights. After putting a small weight on the end of the line, I then fish with a crappie rig that consists of two drop lines coming off a mainline. I usually fish four to six-pound test Berkley XL which, due to its limpness, helps me feel a strike better.

When I fish with a 10- or 11-foot B & M graphite pole, I rig with a crappie hook, a small shot lead and a quill cork and set the cork on the outside edges of the light. Usually I fish two poles and one rod. My fishing companion generally will have the same number of lines down that I do.

Many crappiers use lanterns, either floating lights that shine a beam down deep toward the bottom or a lantern that draws in bugs and allows the bugs to fall into the water. Personally, I utilize both kinds of lights to make sure I'm fishing the right way.

I like to bait with live, large, shiner minnows. My personal experience has been that the bigger the minnows I fish, the larger the crappie I'll catch. However, I also carry at least half-dozen 1/24- and 1/32-ounce jigs with me. Then if I run out of minnows or my minnows start to die when the crappie begin to bite, I still have bait to fish.

WHERE TO FISH FOR NIGHTTIME CRAPPIE

During the summer months, crappie are looking for cool, highly oxygenated water near structure. When the water temperature heats up, the fish often will be found on the edges of a river channel or a deep creek channel. Often the very best place to locate crappie schooled-up during the summer months is on the point formed where a creek channel runs into a river channel. If this spot also has stumps and logs on it, then you'll often find a summertime, nighttime, crappie hotspot.

Crappie may travel these river and creek channels much like motorists travel interstate highways. These areas are where the most baitfish will be found, and the crappie will follow the bait. When you concentrate the baitfish with a light, crappie traveling along these channels will come in to feed when they see the light and the large numbers of baitfish.

If you don't have a depth sounder or a lake map that shows underwater river and creek channels, you still can find the creek and river channel drop-offs and ledges where crappie concentrate during the summer months. Bridges and railroad trestles which cross creeks, rivers and lakes usually effectively concentrate nighttime crappie. The pilings that stand along the edges or in the middles of underwater creek or river channels offer structure for the crappie to hold on as well as provide a place for baitfish to hold.

Also, generally some current is present around pilings. The crappie can hold on the down-current side of the pilings in the slack water and then move out into the current to feed. Too, the pilings offer vertical structure which allows the crappie to position themselves close to cover in the segment of water with the most comfortable temperature as well as the most dissolved oxygen. On many lakes throughout the nation, the area under bridges may resemble a small village at night and on weekends where from 10 to 100 boats may be lined up under the bridges with all the fishermen angling for slabs.

One of the advantages associated with night fishing in many lakes is your inability to communicate to the fish that crappie is the only species you're attempting to catch. Often at night, you will take largemouth bass, smallmouth bass, striped bass, hybrid striped bass, white bass and an occasional bluegill and catfish while crappie fishing. Many species of fish travel these river ledges and drop-offs. When you concentrate the baitfish with a light, generally you also will draw in other species of fish besides crappie to that light.

Another advantage of night fishing for crappie is the fact that many states permit a two-day limit for anglers who fish all

Nighttime fishing for crappie can be fun for the whole family.

night. Conceivably you can catch one limit of crappie before 12:00 midnight as well as another limit of crappie before daylight the next morning. However, this type of regulation is a state-by-state call. Check with the conservation officer in your state to learn what the regulations are for night fishing on the lakes you plan to angle.

HOW CRAPPIE POSITION THEMSELVES AT NIGHT

On the night I fished with Hodnett and Sharman, we caught crappie from two feet off the bottom to two inches below the surface.

"Often the crappie will be holding right on the edge of a break near the bottom," Sharman said. "As the baitfish concentrate under the light closer to the surface, the crappie will move up in the water. Many times you can see them swim into the light and take the bait just beneath the surface. That's

83

why I drop my line all the way to the bottom and then count each turn of the reel off the bottom until I get a bite. The crappie usually will hold at one spot for some time.

"For instance, if I start catching crappie five turns off the bottom, then when I catch a fish next, I immediately bait again, drop my line to the bottom and reel five turns off the bottom. When the crappie stop biting at that depth, I'll drop my bait all the way to the bottom and begin to slowly reel up, counting the turns I'm taking on my reel as I bring my bait up toward the surface. The longer I fish at night, usually the higher up in the water the crappie will be. Many nights just before daylight, all you'll have to do is simply hook a minnow and drop it over the side of the boat to catch fish in one to two feet of water over a 15-foot bottom."

Another interesting feature about night crappie fishing is several different schools may come under the lights at various times of the night. Often you may fish for three or four hours without ever getting a bite and then start catching crappie on every rod as fast as you can get baits in the water for 45 minutes to an hour. Another hour to 1-1/2 hours may pass without getting a bite. Then as quickly as the catching has stopped, it may begin again and often last for only five to 15 minutes or as long as three or four hours.

One reason I enjoy crappie fishing at night in the summertime is it doesn't interfere with any of my daytime activities. I can fish in the afternoon after work, or I can fish all night Friday, all day Saturday and still have Sunday to clean fish and recover.

If you've never given nighttime crappie fishing a try, do it this summer. But I must warn you, nighttime crappie fishing is one of the most addictive forms of fishing I know. Crappie fishing at night in the summer is cool, relaxing, usually rewarding and an ideal way to spend quality time with friends and family away from the rest of the world.

- 9 -

WHY FISH IN 100-DEGREE HEAT

"The hotter the day, and the brighter the sun, the better crappie fishing will be," Dr. Omar Smith of Memphis, Tennessee, says. The Crappie Doctor, as Dr. Smith, a college professor and scientist at Memphis State University is known, has learned tactics that may confound your mind but also will demonstrate his analytical and scientific nature. Using Doc Smith's secret summertime techniques for taking crappie, you can catch crappie all summer long in the middle of the day even in 100-degree weather, if you can find the right kind of lake to fish.

"The most productive lakes for fishing during the hottest part of the summer with the most success often will be oxbow lakes off main river systems," Dr. Smith explains. "Also farm ponds and lakes found in woods where the bottom depth is about the same throughout the body of water will pay crappie dividends.

"If crappie are in a lake, then during the hottest part of the day, they are looking for cover and cool water temperatures. If the water depth is about the same throughout a lake, then the water temperature all across a lake will be similar, which eliminates water temperature as a critical factor in locating crappie in these types of lakes. Cover and shade become the most important ingredients for finding slab-sized crappie.

Dr. Omar Smith of Memphis, Tennessee, is known as the Crappie Doctor who catches slabs in 100-degree weather.

"During the night, crappie tend to spread out in a lake. Even as the sun begins to come up, the crappie still don't have to fight the sun's rays. But when the sun is at its zenith between 10:00 a.m. and 2:00 p.m., the fish must find some type of shade or cover and then concentrate in it.

"Out in the centers of some of the oxbow lakes I fish grow live cypress trees, which provide shade and cover in two different places. Obviously, the first place shade will appear around a cypress tree is at the trunk where you will find crappie holding in that shade and relating to the trunk of the tree."

But if the crappie aren't around the trunk, Doc Smith is not stumped. Because he is familiar with the way a cypress tree grows, he knows that coming out from the stump of the tree below the water is a doughnut-shaped root system.

"If the crappie aren't close to the trunk, then I fish three to four feet away from the trunk on either side of the dough-nut-shaped root system," Doc Smith reports. "The advantage to fishing in the middle of the day is that with the sun straight up overhead, the most shade from the tree will be right under the tree at the trunk or immediately under the root system all the way around the tree. When the sun is rising or setting, the shade shifts to either side of a tree, which allows the crappie to hold in the shade well away from the tree. That's why I

86

catch most of my fish and particularly the biggest crappie I take in the middle of the day."

Doc Smith also is quick to say that other factors influence the success of his crappie fishing in the hot summer like the barometric pressure and the amount of wind on the lake on the day he fishes.

"Moon phase also is very important in determining whether or not you'll be successful -- not only in the summertime but at any season of the year you fish," Smith comments. "I've found that crappie bite better during the week of the full moon. I believe when the sun and the moon are in equal proportions to each other or close to equal proportions to each other that fish, animals and yes, even people are much more comfortable and tend to move and feed better.

"I have learned the most productive fishing is two to three days before and/or after a full moon. When a full moon shines, I feel there is less pressure exerted on the earth by both the sun and the moon. Then the fish tend to bite better."

Another factor the Crappie Doctor has researched about crappie is the time of day the fish bite better under full moon conditions.

"When the moon is full, crappie tend to bite better between 10:00 a.m. and 12:00 noon than they do early in the morning," Smith explains. "Perhaps this happens because the fish feed more actively at night during a full moon than they will if the moon is dark."

With this knowledge and realizing that crappie tend to concentrate under trees in oxbow lakes in the middle of the day to find both shade and cover, then the Crappie Doctor has deduced that on the morning after a full moon, the fish will be feeding between 10:00 a.m. and 12:00 noon, and in the summertime when the sun is hot, the fish must concentrate under the trees standing out in the water. Therefore the most productive time to catch crappie in the summertime in oxbow lakes is the morning after a full moon between 10:00 a.m. and 12:00 noon.

Doc Smith also believes wind blowing on a lake can and will help crappie to bite.

"When the wind blows, and the waves break on a lake, that breaking action of the waves oxygenates the top layer of

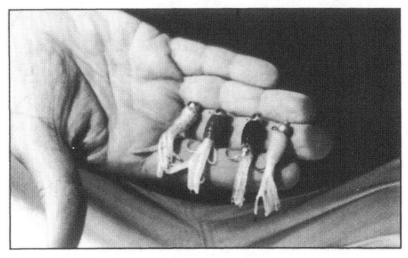

Smith believes the solid-bodied, skirted jigs like those made by Hog Rustler are the most effective for taking crappie consistently.

the water," Smith mentions. "Because that water is more highly oxygenated, the crappie are more comfortable in their environment. I've found that usually they will bite better then."

The Crappie Doctor also is particular about the kind of tackle he uses and prefers eight to 10 foot B & M graphite jig poles because of their lightness. Too, Smith can move these poles easier under the cypress trees than he can longer poles. He also likes six-pound test Trilene clear line since he's fishing so shallow. He is convinced the crappie can see the line if he uses a heavier line.

Smith uses Hog Rustler solid-bodied skirts on his lead-headed jigs because, "These skirts will get numbers of strikes from both crappie and bluegill, which also concentrate under these cypress trees. If you're fishing a hollow tube body jig, then when a bream hits, the fish either will pull the hollow skirt down or off the jig head. But when you're fishing with a solid-bodied skirt, the bream can't pull the skirt down or off. Too, the hollow tube type skirts get destroyed easily when you're catching numbers of crappie. However, I've fished all day long before with a Hog Rustler solid-bodied skirt, caught

88

Fishing oxbow lakes in 100-degree weather can produce slabs like these.

a limit of crappie and still used that same solid-bodied skirt again the next day. I also believe that because the body of the jig is solid and the skirt is hollow, I get more action from the skirt than if I use a hollow tube type body."

For the head of the jig, the Crappie Doctor either will utilize a 1/16- or a 1/32-ounce jig head.

"When the crappie are inactive in the hot summertime, I have found they prefer a smaller, slower moving bait than what they'll take in the spring and fall when the weather is cooler, and they tend to be more active," Smith explains.

When selecting color, the Crappie Doctor prefers black and white, black and chartreuse, black with metal flakes and red and chartreuse jigs.

"To take more crappie if the crappie are biting slowly and are not as active as I wish they were, I've learned to hook a live minnow behind the jig and the solid-bodied skirt," Smith reports. "Often I'll increase the number of strikes I get and the number of fish I catch.

"A new development in bait buckets that helps my minnows to stay alive and livelier for a longer time in 100-degree weather is the Bait-Up II bait bucket. This bucket features a lid that when lifted has a scoop on it that picks up the minnows, brings them to the surface, allows the water to drain off into the bucket and lets you choose the minnow you want to fish with without your having to use a dipnet or put your hand into the bucket to catch a minnow. Dipnets can pick up foreign odors and smells. Your hands also may carry amino acids, especially when you sweat, and may have other foreign substances on them that, when introduced to the minnows' water, may contaminate the water and cause the minnows to become sick or die.

"By using a bucket like the BaitUp II and this baiting system, then I eliminate many of the problems associated with fishing live bait. I also present a better looking minnow to the crappie than anglers do who use dip nets or reach into their buckets with their hands.

"Another critical factor to finding and catching crappie in the summer is the amount of pH in the water. I believe the perfect pH for finding and catching crappie is between 6.5 and 7.5. When you can locate the preferred pH of crappie in a lake during the summer months, and you fish in the middle of the day the day after a full moon at night, then you have combined many of the factors that tend to produce successful crappie fishing during the hot summer months."

One of the reasons Dr. Omar Smith consistently catches more crappie than many other anglers is because he studies weather, water and wind conditions, he knows where the crappie must be according to the time of the day, and he puts a bait in front of them they will take. He maximizes his fishing effort to spend quality time on the water when his chances of catching crappie are best. By approaching crappie fishing more scientifically, the Crappie Doctor takes more slabs than those of us who don't. Knowledge of the crappie, their habits and their habitat will produce more of them more often each day you fish than fishing your lucky spot or with what you believe to be a magic lure.

- 10 -

WHY COLOR IS THE KEY

"What color are you using?" my fishing partner, Alan Padgett asked the two anglers in the other boat after they had landed eight, slab-sized crappie in the same amount of time as we had caught two speckled-sides about three fingers wide each.

"Red/green/yellow," came the reply.

We immediately changed to red/green/yellow and began to take big slabs like the anglers in the boat next to us. Crappie fishermen have their own language. The word color refers to the color of jig a fisherman is casting. Red/green/yellow denotes the tri-colors of the head, the body and the tail of the jig.

That day, I learned how critical fishing the correct jig color is -- not only to catch crappie but to take big crappie. I had been a skeptic. I did not believe in magic potions, secret baits or lucky rods. I knew that locating fish and an angler's skill were required to take crappie. I could not believe that the color of a jig determined whether or not crappie hit and that the color could determine the size of crappie taken.

However, throughout that day, I witnessed with my own eyes that when we had on the correct color of jig, we caught crappie. If I switched jigs and used a color other than the one the crappie were attacking, I would not get a bite. Once we pinpointed the big crappie color, I often altered the colors to see if I could catch large crappie on another color. I never did.

After much research and trying to disprove that the color of the jig makes a difference in catching crappie, I now am convinced that if you can determine which color of jig crappie will bite, you can catch more and bigger crappie on every outing. But how do you know what color crappie prefer to take and when to change colors? I asked three of the nation's leading crappie anglers.

RANDY SULLIVAN -- CRAPPIE GUIDE

Randy Sullivan of Rockwell, Texas, a guide on Lake Fork reservoir, explains that, "Several years ago I was fishing Lake Ray Hubbard catching crappie on either a white or a red and white jig. I noticed the water color started to change and become stained when the water was being pulled from Lake Lavon upstream. Soon the crappie quit biting. Eventually I couldn't see my jigs in the water as well as I had before. I changed from white/red/white to black and black chartreuse colored jigs, and the crappie began to feed actively again.

"I believe dark-colored jigs are easier for the fish to see in dark-colored water than light-colored jigs are. Because crappie feed by sight, the easier the jig is for the fish to spot, the more likely the crappie is to bite."

In clear water, Sullivan favors fishing lighter colored jigs.

"If crappie quit hitting a particular color, then I will fish either a darker or a lighter shade of that same color of jig to try and get the fish to start biting again," Sullivan says.

Sullivan uses a two-step approach to trigger strikes once crappie quit taking his baits. First he reduces the size and weight of the jighead he utilizes, which reduces the speed at which the jig falls.

"When the crappie slow down in their feeding, I use lighter jigs, which fall slower and make the baits visible to the crappie for a longer time," Sullivan reports. "If I don't increase the number of strikes by reducing the weight of the jig, next I switch the color of the jig."

JOE RATTREE -- AVID ANGLER

Joe Rattree of Centre, Alabama, has fished Weiss Lake on the Georgia/Alabama border most of his life and is con-

The author has learned that the color of jig he fishes often determines the size of crappie he catches.

vinced that proper color selection is second only to finding crappie to fish for them successfully.

"When I'm fishing clear lakes, I use two to four-pound test line and light or pastel-colored jigs such as pale yellows, pinks and greens and faded chartreuse," Rattree reports. "I usually fish 1/24- to 1/32-ounce jigs on these lakes. Crappie won't chase a bait far. By using light line and little jigs on a light action rod like a B & M Crappie Rod, you can make a slow lure presentation that will trigger strikes. You must have a light action rod to cast little line and light jigs.

"In clear water, you rarely if ever see dark-colored baitfish. The baitfish often are more transparent, which helps them hide from predator fish. To catch crappie, you must present the jigs that will be about the same shade of color as the baitfish in a reservoir."

In stained water, Rattree prefers jigs in blacks, yellows and reds. The more stain the water has in it, the darker the jig Rattree fishes.

The crappie's preference for certain jig colors often depends on water clarity.

"I use a tri-colored jig when I fish for crappie," Rattree reports. "I let the crappie tell me what color they want. If I'm trolling for crappie, I may have six lines out with a different color combination of jig on the end of each line. Whichever jig starts catching fish, I change out the other lines and put that color jig on them."

According to Rattree, he can determine which color on the tri-color jig the fish want. "If I'm fishing a red/green/yellow jig and catching crappie, then I'll put out numbers of jigs that have at least one of the colors on them that the crappie are hitting. I may fish a black/red/black, a white/green/white or a blue/yellow/blue. I put the color the crappie are hitting in the center of the other jigs. Then I can tell exactly which color is causing the crappie to strike."

But once Rattree understands what color the fish prefer, he does not fish a solid colored jig.

"For instance, if the crappie tell me they like green best, I use other color combinations with the green. Then if the crappie quit hitting the green jigs, I will have on another color besides the green in which they may be interested. If green is the color the crappie are keying in on and I have a white/green/white jig that is getting a lot of action, if the fish quit biting, I may cast back to them with a jig that has a red head, a white body and a red tail. Using this tactic, I can keep up with the colors the crappie prefer."

Rattree's number one choices of jigs to fish in water not gin-clear or clay-hole muddy are chartreuse and white or chartreuse and yellow.

"In lakes with water that is a fish-green color, most of the baitfish in the lake will have some kind of green cast to them," Rattree observes. "I will use dark jigs like a black jig with either some red or yellow on it in darker, heavily stained water and fish heavier line such as six pound test. Then I will fish small pastel or transparent jigs like smoke colors in gin-clear water as well as use small line."

BRAZ WEBB -- LONGTIME EXPERT CRAPPIER

Braz Webb of Bay Minette, Alabama, catches most of his crappie during severe weather conditions as he explains that, "I find and take the most crappie in August when the weather is about 100 degrees or in January and February when the air temperatures are in the 20s or less. The crappie I catch usually will be holding in some type of structure in about 68-degree water. Once I find the structure and the correct water temperature, then the color of my jigs determines whether or not I will catch those crappie."

Webb has several basic colors he always fishes such as green, blue, pearl and white. He changes the shades of these basic colors depending on water clarity. In clear water, Webb will fish very light shades. He fishes the darker shades and replaces the white or pearl jigs with either browns or blacks in dark water. A new color that has proved successful for him is a jig with a rootbeer-colored body and brown tail.

"Since the root beer-colored jigs often come with a white tail, I use a brown magic marker to change the tail color from white to brown," Webb says.

Webb keeps markers handy in red, blue, dark green, black and yellow in his tackle box so he can alter the color of his jigs as he determines what color jigs the crappie want.

Many times the size of crappie you catch is determined by the color of jigs you fish.

"I like laundry markers because the colors don't wash off as easily as the artist markers do," Webb explains. "I primarily use the markers to change the head colors of the jigs. I may make a white head jig yellow with a magic marker if I'm fishing in clear water. I think adding color to a head or changing the color of the head of a jig may cause a fish to think the bait is bigger.

"During extreme weather conditions, the crappie want to expend less energy and eat bigger baits. That's why I generally fish 1/8- or 1/4-ounce jigs. I believe the larger jigs catch bigger crappie during extreme weather conditions. Normally I fish a jig with a lead head, a rubber body and a feather tail. To make the bait appear bigger, I often will use my markers

If you want to catch big crappie like these, first you must determine what jig colors the crappie in your area prefer.

to change the color of the feather on the end of the jig. If a white feather is on the end of a rubber body, that white feather may make the crappie think the feather is the baitfish's tail. By painting that white feather green to cause it to appear to be an extension of the body of the jig, then the jig looks longer, seems bigger and may be more likely to be eaten by a large crappie."

Webb also will fish a bulky curlytail grub or a tube type jig to make his bait look larger and heavier to interest the bigger crappie.

"If I am catching little crappie on a particular color of jig, I will change my jigs out and use that same color in a larger jig size. Generally I will catch the bigger crappie then."

97

Webb also has developed some theories about where big crappie hold.

"I believe the bigger crappie hold at the bottom of a school," Webb mentions. "If you use larger, heavier jigs, you are more likely to get your baits down to the bigger crappie in the school. I also have learned that the bigger crappie usually will stay on the outside edges of a school and will be the most aggressive."

TOM MANN -- MASTER FISHERMAN

A few years ago, I fished with Tom Mann of Eufaula, Alabama, who is known more as a bass fisherman than a crappie fisherman. Mann is a lure manufacturer, a tournament angler and the person Mama Mann sends out when she wants a mess of crappie to eat.

Tom Mann explained to me that, "I don't know if crappie key in as much on color as most anglers believe they do. But I have found that crappie wise up to color quicker than bass do.

"Often crappie fishermen leave a spot where crappie will continue to bite because they don't switch the colors of the jigs they're fishing. When crappie quit biting, they still may be in a feeding mode but have noticed that some of the fish in their school vanish when they see a certain color of jig. The crappie quickly learn that when that color jig comes into the school they better leave it alone or they will vanish too. However, when a new color falls into the school, that color doesn't have a past history with that group of fish. They may bite it more readily than a color they already have seen."

Why do crappie prefer one color over another? The reasons are as varied as the number of anglers who fish for them. However, successful crappie fishermen have learned that when they choose the color of jig crappie prefer, they can catch more slabs on that color jig than any other jigs in their tackle boxes.

When you are fishing but not catching crappie, do not assume the crappie are not biting. Continue to alter the colors of the jigs you are fishing until you discover the right color to flip the crappie's feeding switch from off to on.

- 11 -

HOW TO TROLL FOR CRAPPIE

Editor's Note: David Stancil of Tennessee is one of the nation's most well-recognized crappie fishing pros who has been very successful in many crappie tournaments through the years. In this chapter, he shares many of his secrets.

The weather was rough, the fishing was bad, and the chances of catching a crappie were slim. My partner, Mike Howard of Oxford, Alabama, and I were with some of the best crappie fishermen in the world who had assembled at Lake Weiss on the Alabama/Georgia border for the U.S. Crappie National Championship in 1989. On this day, anglers not only had to do battle with one another but also with Mother Nature.

We found our fish out on a creek channel in the middle of the lake where we spotted them on our depthfinders. Then we slowly trolled through the crappie. We won that championship because we caught the most and biggest crappie by using three depthfinders and adjusted the depth and the speed at which we were fishing to allow our jigs to troll through the crappie we saw on the screens.

That is one of the advantages of trolling for crappie. You can adapt your fishing pattern from one end of the boat to the other. If you miss the fish with the jigs being trolled by the front rods, you can change the depth at which the jigs are trolling and take crappie at the back of the boat.

David Stancil has learned the secrets of trolling for crappie. His success earned him the 1989 U.S. Crappie National Championship.

The first time I ever trolled for crappie was in the early 1980s when I was fishing with a friend, Robbie Hurst, at Lake Pymatuning in Pennsylvania at a crappie tournament. We had heard from some of the other pros about trolling for crappie. On the first competition day, we went to a spot where we had found crappie the day before, but the fish were not there. We decided to try this new tactic called trolling.

I held one rod in each hand, and Robbie held one rod in each hand. As we moved the boat around the point where we had located crappie the day before, we started catching plenty of crappie. When a fish hit, I set the hook and put the rod that did not have a fish on it between my legs while I reeled in the rod that had the fish. Even though I knew little about this trolling tactic, when I saw how effective it was, I realized I had to learn more about fishing like that. We caught crappie all day long by trolling that first time.

When you troll for crappie, you cover more water with more jigs than you will if you stay in one place and catch fish. Because Mike Howard and I catch large numbers of crappie, we generally take the bigger fish in a lake. Although we may not catch three and four pound crappie trolling, we usually will have more 1-1/2- to 1-3/4-pound crappie than anyone else fishing on a lake. Here are 10 keys I have pinpointed that help us to regularly locate the fish.

UTILIZE DEPTHFINDERS

I consider a depthfinder second only to my boat in importance for me to find and take crappie. A depthfinder tells me where the fish are situated, on what type of structure, how deep the water is where the fish are holding, how fast I need to run my trolling motor to pull my jigs through the fish and when the fish move.

Mike and I may begin trolling for crappie early in the morning and see on the depthfinder that the fish are holding at 20-feet deep. By 10:00 a.m., the crappie may have moved up to 12 feet of water. If we are still running our jigs at 20 feet, our baits will be passing under the fish. Crappie will not go down to take baits. Knowing exactly where the fish are positioned in the water tells us how to fish.

We have three depthfinders on our boat -- a flasher, a Humminbird LCR and a Bottom Line graph. But still you can catch plenty of crappie by only using one depthfinder. We like a flasher on the front end of the boat because the flasher gives us the signal back from the bottom quicker than an LCR does. We mount our flasher to the foot of the trolling motor on the front of the boat to get the quickest picture of the bottom first. With a flasher, we realize instantly what is under the boat. By the time an LCR shows us a picture of the bottom, we may be 10 to 15 feet away from the fish we are spotting on the screen. The flasher also pinpoints bottom

Utilizing a depth finder to pinpoint productive crappie spots is essential for success.

breaks. Then we can buoy off a creek channel or a river ledge we want to fish.

Behind the flasher, we usually have a Humminbird LCR to allow us to look at the structure and fish the flasher does not show us. Then, mounted on the console of the boat is a Bottom Line graph, which has a graph line feature a Humminbird LCR does not. This graph draws the bottom like a paper graph and provides much more detailed information than any LCR.

By the time crappie vanish off my LCR, they will start to appear on the Bottom Line console depthsounder Mike is watching. If I fail to get a bite, Mike quickly and easily either can change the color of his jigs or reel in or let out his lines. Then his jigs will pass either more shallow in the water than my jigs or deeper in the water than mine if he lets out line. Often the fisherman in the back of the boat will take crappie the angler on the front of the boat never catches. We know that using three depthfinders is very important to our success.

A depthfinder is only half the key to locating crappie. You also have to understand where to look for the fish and have an idea of where the crappie should be. Our primary target for trolling for crappie is the edges of creek channels with cover on them because crappie are structure- oriented fish. At certain times of the year, however, you will find crappie in the middle of a lake or a creek channel not holding on or in the cover. But the crappie will be holding close to cover and not far from it.

Even in the spring of the year when most people are fishing the bank, Mike and I troll creek channels. Many anglers do not understand that the biggest concentration of crappie will be on a creek channel on any lake -- even during the spring spawn. Generally, the very big crappie will not go into shallow water to spawn but rather will be holding in eight to 10 feet of water, most often near the cover on the creek channels.

UNDERSTAND THE SEASONAL MIGRATION PATTERNS OF CRAPPIE

The second key to finding crappie to catch when you are trolling is you must know the seasonal migration patterns of the fish. During the pre-spawn before crappie move onto creek channels, they usually will concentrate in the mouths of creeks where they will be waiting on warmer water to trigger the spawn in the creeks. When the spawn begins, most of the crappie in any creeks will be found from 3/4 of the way into the creek to the back of the creek.

Then, immediately after the spawn during the post-spawn, generally, the crappie will move back to a creek channel and be holding on points and underwater structure about halfway from the mouth of a creek to the back of a creek. Deep creek channels and the bends of main river channels are the preferred sites for crappie during hot summer months.

In the fall, the crappie once again will repeat their spring pattern by being in the same spots they have been in the pre-spawn and post-spawn -- the mouths of creeks and halfway between the mouths and the backs of creeks. The fall crappie, however, will not go into that very shallow water as they do in the spring.

103

As soon as the water first changes from warm to cool, the crappie will be in the mouths of creeks. When the weather becomes somewhat colder, they will start to move from the mouths of creeks toward the backs of the creeks. When the weather gets very cold, the crappie swim out of the creeks and head toward deeper water.

DETERMINE THE COLOR OF JIGS TO FISH

The third key to taking crappie when trolling is learning what color of jigs the crappie prefer on that day. When many anglers crappie fish, they only may utilize a yellow, a chartreuse or a white jig. But Mike and I carry 54 various colors of jigs with us. Determining what color of jig crappie will bite on any given day is critical to your success when trolling, since the crappie only may bite one particular color for two hours. Mike and I have learned that the color of the water, the brightness of the day, the time of the year, the water temperature and the individual lake where we are fishing all seem to affect the colors of jigs the crappie prefer on any given day.

For instance, the crappie may hit a jig with a white head, a blue body and a white feathered tail. When they stop biting this color, they may prefer a jig with a red head, a yellow body and a yellow tail. Trolling will let you know when this change occurs. We like to fish jigs with a lead head, a soft rubber body and a maribou tail.

My partner and I troll with 14 rods out in states where no limit exists on the number of rods an angler can fish at one time. Each rod has a different color jig on it. Once a color starts catching crappie, we will change out all our jigs to that color. If the fish are hitting solid black jigs, all 14 rods will troll black jigs. If the fish quit biting, but we still can see the crappie on our depthfinders, then we start switching colors. Depending on what color the fish are hitting, we once again will change jigs. Whether or not you are fishing two rods or 14 rods, let the crappie tell you what color of jigs to fish as well as when to change colors.

Usually, we catch the most fish trolling jigs weighing either 1/24- or 1/16-ounce. When the crappie are not feeding actively, they seem to prefer the smaller jigs. If the fish are biting aggressively, we fish the heavier jigs.

Anglers may put out many rods for crappie, but the ability to read a depthfinder is what often makes the difference between success or failure.

CHOOSE CORRECT LINE SIZE

Fishing with the correct line size is the fourth key to catching crappie while trolling. The size of line you troll will determine how deep your jigs swim.

Heavier pound-test line is more buoyant than smaller pound test line. If the water is clear, and the fish are deep, we troll four pound test Trilene XT line. The smaller line enables a bait to get deeper, which is where fish will be located in clear water but is difficult for the fish to see -- even in clear water. However, if the water is stained, we can fish heavier six pound test line, because generally the fish will be more shallow, and they still will not be able to spot the line. We never fish line heavier than six pound test. We prefer the XT because it is more abrasion-resistant. We need abrasion resistance more than castability when we are trolling.

PLACE RODS PROPERLY

The fifth key to successfully taking crappie is proper rod position. The way you position your rods often determines how many fish you can catch out of a school of crappie, how quickly you can land the fish, and whether or not you will tangle your lines.

In a rod holder on the front of the boat, we place a 5-1/2-foot rod with a rod holder bent down as close as we can get it to the water without it actually touching the water. The second rod on the same side of the boat is an eight foot rod. We have the rod holder bent as the line from this rod will run just above the line coming from the 5-1/2-foot rod. The third rod is 11 feet long. We bend the rod holder with the 11-foot rod so its line is held just above the line from the eight foot rod.

With three rods on the right hand side of the boat and three on the left hand side of the boat, I can cover 26 to 28 feet of water at a time. My partner in the back of the boat also has three rods out the left hand side and three rods out the right hand side stacked the same way besides two rods coming off the stern of the boat. Positioning our rods in this way not only keeps the lines separated, but, also, when we get a crappie on any rod, the lines are far enough apart that we can reel in the crappie without tangling the fish in the other lines.

We fish with B & M graphite rods, which have a light tip action, yet plenty of strength to land the crappie. We also use Zebco ultralight spinning reels, which have drag systems that feed line off evenly under pressure. Then we do not lose the crappie that hit our jigs.

USE A HEAVY DUTY TROLLING MOTOR

The sixth key to trolling for crappie is using our MotorGuide Brute Competition 45-pound thrust, 24-volt trolling motor with a continuous gear amp, which means we can run the motor constantly for a long time. When we are trolling, we never stop the trolling motor, no matter what. With this particular trolling motor, we can troll continuously for eight to nine hours per day for two days without having to charge the battery.

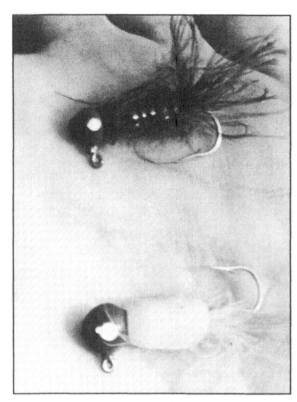

David Stancil turns the hook of his jig to face the opposite way from where it has been designed to face to reduce the number of hangups.

Mike and I need the 45-pound thrust this motor has because, as the fishing day progresses, often wind becomes a factor in our ability to catch big crappie. Although we try not to troll against the wind, sometimes we have to go into the wind to reach a spot to stall our jigs so they will fall deep to catch bigger crappie. If we do not have enough power in our trolling motor to buck the wind at the speed we need to troll to get our jigs down, we will not be able to take the bigger and better-sized crappie.

LEARN THE ADVANTAGES OF A
TEMPERATURE GAUGE

The seventh key to catching crappie by trolling is utilizing a temperature gauge. For example, in a creek in the early spring, the surface temperature at the mouth of the creek may be 55 degrees. But the further back into the creek you go, and the warmer the water gets, the closer you will be to finding crappie.

Mike and I have learned the ideal water temperature for catching crappie in the spring is 65 to 70 degrees. Even if the fish are in a pre-spawn condition, and we know because of the time of year the crappie should be in the mouths of creeks, we still will fish the backs of these creeks where the water temperature is warmer. Although crappie are structure-oriented, they are more temperature-oriented. Even if plenty of structure is in the mouth of a creek with a water temperature of 55 degrees, we will fish the back of the creek with very little structure where the water temperature is 65 degrees.

UNDERSTAND THE PROPER HOOK SET
AND DRAG SET

The eighth key to catching more crappie by trolling is hook set and drag set. I set the drag on my reel by pulling the line straight out from the rod until the drag begins to slip, and the line does not break. If you are fighting a big crappie, and one of your jigs gets hooked in the structure, you must make a decision as to whether to land the fish, snap the line or break the rod if your drag is set too tight. However, if you set the drag loose enough, the line will peel off the reel evenly, although the jig gets hooked in the structure. Then you can land your fish. Once the crappie is in the boat, you either can pull the jig free or break it off.

Many people who troll for crappie let the fish set the hooks themselves. We may use this tactic when we are in a large school of crappie. However, if we can set the hooks on fish, we generally try and set the hooks ourselves rather than depending on the power of the boat to do it. We believe we get a better hook set and catch more crappie when we jerk the rods and set the hooks.

REPOSITION THE HOOK

The ninth key to catching more crappie is altering the jig so it does not hang in the structure as often as it normally will. Some anglers will not troll regions with numerous stumps and

Proper trolling techniques can result in an impressive catch!

brush because they lose so many jigs. To prevent losing so many jigs, we turn the hook 180 degrees to face the opposite way from how it has been designed to face. The hook runs under the eye of the jig instead of above the eye of the jig. Then, the jig will tend to bounce off the cover better, gets hung less and produces more fish.

I learned about turning the hooks from my fishing buddy, Robbie Hurst, on a trip we made in the early 80s when we were casting and retrieving jigs in a sunken treetop but hanging up constantly. Then Robbie turned his hook around and did not get hung up, even after two or three casts. After turning my hook around, I had more success with not becoming hung in the cover. Later, I incorporated this jig modification into my trolling tactic.

109

PLACE MINNOWS AS TRAILERS ON JIGS

The tenth key to trolling and taking crappie is to realize that even though trolling jigs is the deadliest method of catching crappie, on some days the fish just will not hit any jig -- no matter what the color. That is when we troll jigs and use live minnows as trailers, a strategy we learned in the 1989 U.S. Crappie National Championship.

We had located crappie in deep water just off a point where the water temperature was 80 degrees. But the fish seemed to have lockjaw. Even when we got our jigs down to them, we could not make the big crappie bite.

We began using small pieces of shot lead about 18 to 20 inches up the lines and lip-hooked small shiner minnows on the ends of floating jigs. The floating jigs kept the minnows from dragging the bottom and helped them appear more lifelike. By trolling the jigs with the small minnows on them over those deep water crappie, we were able to get the fish to bite and win the tournament.

This tactic is very deadly during the post-spawn. Fishing a jig with a live shiner minnow lip-hooked on it usually means we catch 10 crappie to every one we will have caught if we are fishing just the jig. Once you know where to find crappie, how to troll for them and what baits to use to catch these fish, you will be able to catch crappie at any time of the year under any weather and water conditions.

- 12 -

HOW TO JIGPOLE FISH
FOR CRAPPIE

If you fish visible cover with a pole, sooner or later, you will become a jigpole fisherman.

I realized this a few years ago when I was catching big slab crappie on minnows in standing timber, and a fate worse than death happened. I ran out of minnows. I had to make one of the most critical decisions in the history of my crappie fishing. Did I go home with the fish I'd caught and leave the crappie biting? Or, should I continue to fish with nothing but a jig on the end of my line?

I'd always used jigs with ultralight spinning tackle when trying to cover a lot of water and the crappie were on scattered stumps during the spawn. I'd also fished with a jig and a cork for spring crappie making a spawning run. But I'd never replaced minnows with jigs when I'd found crappie in visible cover. However, on this day, the choice I had to make was obvious. I tried jigpole fishing and became addicted to it.

Even when I'm using minnows, if I locate schooled-up crappie, I'll switch to jigpole fishing. Four of the best jigpole fishermen in the nation share their techniques.

GARY BRAZEALE -- TOURNAMENT ANGLER

The Arkansas tournament crappie fisherman has won the award of Angler-of-the-Year in his state.

"I believe that because of the sensitivity of the jigpole, I can feel a strike better than I can on a rod," Brazeale com-

Jigpole fishing produces slabs at any time of the year under any weather conditions and around any type of structure.

ments. "I also know I'm not nearly as limited with a pole as I am when fishing with a rod. With a rod, you can cast your jig only into certain places without getting hung. However, with a jigpole, I can put my bait through a one inch hole in any bush or treetop where I believe crappie are holding. The jigpole allows anglers to fish every possible part of the visible cover.

"I use six-pound test line on my jigpole and only fish vertically. When I'm not fishing visible cover, I fish submerged cover on drop-offs or deep channels. In the summertime, I'll be fishing in 12 to 15 feet of water. In the wintertime, I'll fish in 15 to 20 feet of water. Then, as the weather begins to heat up or cool down, I follow the fish into the shallows."

112

Brazeale utilizes his jigpole tactics when he's fishing stumps and trees under the surface just as he does when he's fishing stumps and trees he can see. By learning to feel what the jig is touching under the surface, an experienced jigpole fisherman can work segments of underwater cover that an angler who casts and retrieves, trolls or even minnow fishes can't. During the colder months, Brazeale has found larger jigs usually produce bigger crappie.

"Cold water fish bite slow," Brazeale reports. "If you put a big jig in front of a small crappie, the fish usually won't take the bait. But, if a large crappie spots a bait it can catch and eat easily and quickly without expending much energy, the fish will take the bigger jig in that thick cover.

"When I fish crappie tournaments in the wintertime, I first use the small jigs to catch a limit of crappie and then the big jigs to take the larger fish. Then I cull the smaller ones. Wintertime is one of the most productive seasons to fish vertically using a jigpole. I've busted ice with my boat during the winter and still caught huge stringers of big crappie.

"I've also found that, after an hour or so of fishing one school, the fish will be three to four feet shallower than when I first started catching them. Perhaps crappie in a school follow the hooked fish up toward the surface."

DAVID CLARK -- AVID ANGLER

David Clark of Lincoln, North Carolina, has finished in the top three for the last three years in all the tournaments he has fished and has qualified for the Crappiethon Classic all three years.

"I believe I catch more fish with a jigpole than with minnows," he says. "Also, I eliminate having to keep the minnows alive. I probably can catch 100 crappie on one jig without breaking it off. Using a jigpole means I can take more crappie on fewer jigs. However, in very heavy cover, I may take only three or four fish per jig before the it breaks off."

If Clark is fishing isolated cover, he casts the jig out next to the cover and counts the jig down to locate the water depth at which the fish are feeding.

"I use a 1/32-ounce jig and line no larger than four pound test on my jigpole," Clark explains. "I have a spinning reel on my B & M jigpole. Using this jig and line combination, I know my jig falls approximately one foot per second. If the crappie are holding in one foot of water, when the jig hits the water, I say, "1,001," and start reeling. If the fish are holding in three feet of water, I count to three and start my retrieve."

Clark uses his pole like a long rod. Although the most common way to fish a jigpole is to swim the jig close to cover, he also utilizes a form of jigpoling to fish bridge pilings.

"I pitch the jig out and let it fall on a slack line," Clark mentions. "I watch my Humminbird depthfinder to learn at what depth the fish are holding. As the jig falls, I count it down. As the line comes off my reel, I let it barely touch my index finger, which causes the jig to jump slightly and sends off a vibration I believe triggers a strike by the crappie. If the fish are in 40 to 50 feet of water, I'll put a piece of No. 3 split shot 10 to 12 inches up my line. Then my jig can get down to the depths easier and quicker, and I can start my retrieve."

Most crappie anglers understand that color is a critical factor causing crappie to bite. Clark believes using the right color on his jigpole is one reason he catches about 2,000 crappie a year from his home lake, Lake Norman.

"I use the Multi-C-Lector by Lake Systems to determine what jig color I should be using and eliminate guesswork."

GERALD CONLEE -- CRAPPIE RECORD HOLDER

Gerald Conlee of Fernando, Mississippi, broke the Mississippi State Record for black crappie in March, 1991 with a crappie that weighed four pounds, four ounces. The fish also was recognized as a world's record for six pound test line by the National Freshwater Fishing Hall of Fame.

"Because jigs are easier to handle than minnows, and I don't feel I get hung up as much using jigs, I rely on jigpole tactics to catch crappie," Conlee reports. "I'm also convinced that the more water you cover, the more crappie you take. Using a jigpole means I can cover more water faster."

The world's record tactic that Conlee favors is so simple most crappie fishermen rarely utilize it.

"Most of the time, I fish blown-down trees or brush," Conlee comments. "I find an eddy with this type of cover and drop my jig straight down in the water beside the cover. Then

Red Cotton of West Point, Mississippi, is the ultimate master of the jigpole.

I reel the jig back to the surface. Sometimes I may move the jig back and forth or up and down. But many anglers don't realize that the B & M poles I use are so sensitive that the boat motion alone causes the jig to rise and fall. I try and keep the boat just at pole's length from the structure to avoid spooking the crappie."

Conlee uses a Lowrance depthfinder and primarily fishes the Coldwater River of North Mississippi.

"Although I'll fish in any depth of water where I find the crappie holding, I most often pinpoint crappie in 10 to 12 feet of water," he says. "I use a 1/8-ounce jig -- usually black and chartreuse -- on six pound test line because the water I'm fishing remains stained all year. I believe a black jig produces more crappie in stained water than other colors do."

Conlee has a simple approach to jigpole fishing. He mentions to remember that...

* Crappie hold off the current in eddy areas.

* Crappie prefer some type of structure like blown-down trees or bushes in which to hold.

* Crappie most often will strike a bait that falls vertically by where they're holding.

During the summer, you can fish through water vegetation like lily pads with a jigpole and catch plenty of big crappie.

With a jigpole, Conlee can reach every part of the structure by letting his jig drop vertically through the structure. This method keeps him from getting hung as often as the anglers do who cast and retrieve; it also puts his bait in the strike zone of the crappie longer and keeps him from disturbing the other fish holding in that same cover when he pulls a fish out.

RED COTTON -- MASTER OF THE JIGPOLE

Red Cotton of West Point, Mississippi, believes jigpole fishing is not only an easier way to catch crappie but also that, "You don't lose as many fish when you're jigpole fishing. As soon as the crappie takes the jig, you usually will pull straight up on the line and hook the crappie in the top of their mouths, which is much tougher than the sides of the mouth where the skin is like tissue paper. When I used minnows, most of the crappie I took were caught in the side of the mouth. I lost more fish then than I do now that I'm fishing with a jig pole."

Cotton prefers either a white, yellow or a red and white jig and fishes with either six-pound or 10-pound test Tri-Max

Buck Simmons of West Point, Mississippi, the president of the B & M Company, believes so much in the effectiveness of jigpole fishing that he's developed the Buck's Graphite Crappie Pole.

line and an 11-foot B & M jigpole. Cotton, who jigpole fishes all year long, understands where to locate crappie.

"In the spring, I find crappie around shallow water brush piles in a foot to four feet of water," Cotton mentions. "The fish generally will hold at this depth for three to five weeks. Then the fish will move out from the shallows often over a 20-foot bottom in 10 to 12 feet of water either on or near a drop-off. In the fall, the fish move back into the shallows. As the weather becomes colder, the fish return to deep water. Basically crappie only hold in two different water depths of the lake I fish throughout the year.

"I'm convinced jigpole fishing is effective on crappie because of the crappie's basic, lazy nature. These fish aren't aggressive like bass and won't go out of their ways to attack baits. If you don't put your jig in front of a crappie's nose, it usually won't bite. Jigpole fishing allows me to almost always place the jig to within one to five inches of the crappie's face. Since I've been jigpole fishing for 30 years, I know this way is the most effective to take crappie."

Cotton also likes jigpole fishing because he rarely loses any of his 1/32- or 1/16-ounce jigs, which enables him to "almost wear a jig out before losing it."

One of Cotton's secrets is to fish the cover with three different jig colors. Like a competitive bass angler, he carries more than one jigpole when he's searching for crappie.

"I have three jigpoles with me at all times," Cotton explains. "I tie a white jig on one, a chartreuse jig on another pole and a yellow jig on my third pole. I generally fish with a white jig first around any cover. If I don't get a bite, I'll try chartreuse. If the fish fail to hit that color, I'll go to the yellow jig. If a crappie is on the cover I'm fishing, it usually will take one of those colors."

Using this three-pole tactic, Cotton increases his odds for catching more crappie.

"I've also learned that often you'll take the biggest crappie around isolated sticks or stumps," Cotton explains. "Many times only one or two crappie will be holding on a stick about as big around as your wrist. But the crappie you catch around this isolated cover most often will be big crappie."

Jigpole fishing ...

* allows you to fish your jig vertically through various water depths in even the thickest cover,

* lets you work the cover more thoroughly than when using a cast-and-retrieve method of fishing and

* spooks fewer crappie because you pull the crappie straight up out of the cover instead of dragging that slab through the cover.

These experts have proven jigpole fishing works for them. This technique will produce papermouths for you.

- 13 -

WHY FISH CRANKBAITS FOR CRAPPIE

EDITOR'S NOTE: Perhaps the most underused weapons in the arsenal of the crappie fisherman is the crankbait. Immediately when the word crankbait is mentioned, most anglers assume the fishermen are talking about big, fat, deep-diving bass lures. But a relatively new family of crankbaits that go by the titles of mini, wee, little, teeny or baby has been producing number of papermouths nationwide.

One of the professors in the school of small crankbait fishing for crappie is Joe Hughes of Fort Smith, Arkansas, who teaches the crankbait session for Indiana State's Fishing Institute and also is one of the nation's leading proponents of wee crankbaits for crappie. Public Relations Director for Plastics Research, which includes Rebel, Heddon and Cordell lures, Hughes lists among his favorite, all-time crankbaits for any species of the fish, the Wee-R Crawfish.

I believe that the crankbait is the most underpublicized crappie bait in America today. Few writers are publishing articles about little crankbaits for crappie, even though many anglers fish with them.

Small crankbaits have gained in popularity as fishing pressure on lakes across the country has increased, and the numbers of fish being taken have decreased. One advantage of fishing a small crankbait is that it does not cull any fish. You can catch just about any fish that swims with a wee crankbait. Let's look at when the little crankbait is the most effective for taking crappie and how to fish it for crappie in the most productive waters.

WHEN AND WHERE TO FISH LITTLE CRANKBAITS

Because of their sizes, small crankbaits will not dive to deep depths. They are shallow water lures. They are the most proficient when the crappie are in shallow water, which generally occurs two times in the year -- the fall and the spring. When the crappie are in shallow water, they most often are around, over or in some type of structure.

If an angler throws a big crankbait into that shallow water, many times the lure will dive down and dig into the bottom. But a little crankbait can be reeled slowly. Even though it dives under the water, it can be worked in depths of less than a foot around structure.

Also, little crankbaits like the Wee-R Crawfish or the small minnow type baits will hit a limb or a twig and bounce over them without hanging up because of the lure's small hooks. Some anglers may question the effectiveness of small hooks as opposed to larger hooks. However, the small hooks on little crankbaits will not get hung up as much as big hooks will.

Besides, the most important feature of a hook is how sharp it is. The size of the hook is not necessarily what the angler should be concerned with, but rather how sharp the hook is. The little hooks of the smaller crankbaits are deadly at penetrating the mouths of crappie and holding onto the fish. Something else that fishermen tend to forget is that although the crappie will eat a 4-1/2-inch spoonbill minnow, generally speaking they prefer to feed on smaller baits, like little crawfish and shad, which the wee crankbaits resemble.

But the main advantage to angling with a small crankbait is it allows crappie anglers to cover plenty of water in a short time with a very productive lure. When the crappie are moving in shallow, you can cast the crankbait across the tops of grass flats, down long rows of stumps and around any kind of standing structure and quickly and effectively find those shallow water fish. If you want to fish the lure in deeper water, use two to four pound test line, and the bait will dive about a foot deeper than it will on six- or eight-pound test.

Joe Hughes believes in the power of the little crankbait for crappie.

Yet another advantage to finding the small crankbaits is the angler does not have to be touch-sensitive to catch crappie with them. If you are fishing a very light jig around a treetop or a stump, you must be able to feel when the crappie takes the bait, even if the jig is on the fall when the fish hits. An angler also must be able to tell when the jig is bumping through the structure and not set the hook when the jig drops over a limb. But with a small crankbait, you can fish the periphery or the outside of the structure and call the active crappie out away from the limbs. When the fish attack the bait, there is no question about whether a fish has bitten or if you have struck a limb.

Also small crankbaits land lightly on the water and do not make much of a splash when they hit. Oftentimes when crappie are in these shallow water regions in the summer and fall, if you cast a heavy jig that makes a loud plop, or if you swing a large cork into the area where the crappie are holding, the bait will spook the fish. But usually this problem does not occur with the lighter, plastic crankbaits.

121

HOW TO TROLL CRANKBAITS FOR CRAPPIE

If you are going to troll crankbaits for crappie, which is a proven technique for taking large saddle-blanket-size fish, most of the time you will utilize a medium to small crankbait -- rather than one of the baby crankbaits on the market. The bigger lipped crankbaits, one size larger than the tiny or wee crankbaits, cause a lure to dive deeper and to be more stable in the water, which allows an angler to troll the baits rather than having to use a steady retrieve.

Trolling for crappie is a slow motion sport. If you are trolling for crappie with your 150-horsepower outboard, you are probably trolling way too fast. I have found that if the bait can be trolled between one and 1-1/2 miles per hour, then the lure will reach its maximum depth and be trolled at a speed at which the crappie can take it.

WHY USE BASS BAITS FOR CRAPPIE

The Bass Track Shad Junior, which is about a 1/8-ounce crankbait, is somewhat bigger than the wee crankbaits but is an effective crappie catching lure. Another crankbait that many crappie fishermen never assume is a papermouth bait is the Wee-R. One angler in Austin, Texas, catches about 4,000 crappie a year with the Wee-R. Although most anglers troll the Wee-R, this particular sportsman locates suspended crappie with his depthfinder, casts to these fish with the Wee-R and then cranks through the schools. His catch record is phenomenal.

I think the world of crappie fishing is just now beginning to expand past the jig and minnow tactics to which we are all so accustomed. I believe that as we learn more about crappie and crappie fishing, we will be looking at more traditional bass baits to utilize for locating and taking crappie. I feel that we are also going to see much of the technology we have learned from the competition bass fishermen being transferred over to the crappie angler.

Although this particular Texas fisherman has been highly successful using the Wee-R, I personally feel that the Teeny Wee-R or the Super Teeny Wee-R will catch as many crappie as the Wee-R will. But I just personally like and believe in the

Small crankbaits, can catch some of the biggest crappie in any lake.

small crankbaits. When we are talking about crankbaits and casting or trolling them, remember that the slower these crankbaits can be trolled or retrieved once they reach the maximum depth, the more fish the angler will take.

WHICH COLORS TAKE CRAPPIE

I am convinced that sportsmen are just beginning to scratch the surface on the importance of color in successful crappie fishing. I think crankbaits can and do produce numbers of crappie for the fishermen who learn how to use the lures. But I also realize that the sportsmen who understand which color of crankbait is the best in certain water conditions will catch more crappie than anglers who are merely casting and/or trolling crankbaits.

In clear water, colors like green, red, black, gray, white and pearls seem to be much more productive lures and catch more fish than other colors do. Reds, pinks, chartreuses, limes and chromes will produce more crappie in stained water.

In muddy water, the colors that crappie prefer is anybody's guess, unless the lake is like Lake Eufaula in Oklahoma.

123

Very seldom does that lake clear up. If you are going to fish this lake, you will have to experiment with color until you can determine which one the crappie in that muddy lake will hit.

A large crappie population lives in Oklahoma's Lake Eufaula, and many anglers catch plenty of crappie there. But they know ahead of time they will be fishing in muddy water when they are on this lake and that they will have to experiment with color.

To sum up, anglers know that crankbaits catch crappie, little crankbaits produce many crappie when the fish are in shallow water during the fall and the spring, and color is a critical factor in the effectiveness of any particular crankbait. Also we understand that trolling crankbaits for crappie produces good-sized fish when the crappie are in the mouths of creeks or holding on creek channels or river ledges. We also have learned that casting crankbaits, especially the bigger crankbaits, will produce some big crappie when the fish are suspended. We realize that the anglers throwing the bigger crankbaits like the Wee-R catch more crappie on light line like two- and four-pound test. However, most sportsmen think we are just beginning to develop crankbait technology as it relates to crappie.

Cranking for crappie is one of the newest tactics in the field of panfishing and is one that has been and will continue producing. Hopefully, as we learn more, this method should yield bigger and better crappie for all of us.

- 14 -

WHY AND WHERE GORILLA TACTICS STILL WORK

"Why, when I was your age, I had to walk 20 miles barefoot in a blizzard to get to school," the old timer told me. "We were so poor that in my lunch I had to carry day-old biscuits and honey in a fruit jar. Mama never would let me eat the honey out of the fruit jar. I was just permitted to rub the biscuit up and down the outside of the jar and think I was getting some honey on it to sweeten the biscuit.

"You boys have life much softer than we ever had. Back in the good ole days, you had to be tough to survive."

And crappie fishing in the good old days for me was much different from what it is today. Power, brute force and gorilla-like tactics that employed strong line and poles that resembled pool cues caught crappie in days past in inaccessible places rather than using light lines and high-tech fishing. Today the modern crappie fisherman is so sophisticated often there is very little work or struggle involved in his taking an ice chest full of fish.

I'm not complaining. I like being able to utilize a depthfinder to locate crappie. I enjoy fishing lighter lines and small rods to take bigger fish. Angling out of a comfortable, modern, fiberglass bass boat is much more enjoyable than spending the day in a leaky, flat-bottom aluminum johnboat and sitting on a worn-out cushion. But the old way still works for catching crappie. Some of these gorilla-like methods are ones I learned when crappie was a survival food for most families and not a sportfish and still will work today.

WHERE TO FIND CRAPPIE

To be able to catch more and bigger crappie, just thinking like a crappie is not enough. You also must be able to think like a crappie fisherman. For instance in times past, any visible cover like bushes, treetops and standing timber was the target of the perch jerker. Every bush on a river or lake system during the spring and summer would be decorated with canepole anglers.

But to catch bigger and better crappie, you must fish in areas where the fishing pressure is the least, which eliminates the obvious structure. Today, crappiers have learned to troll the mouths of creeks, creek channels and ditches and fish invisible structure by using their depthfinders. Although this type of cover receives less fishing pressure than visible cover does, I still want to fish remote areas where the big white and black crappie rarely, if ever, see a jig or a minnow. I hunt cutoff creeks, sloughs and inaccessible areas to fish.

When I use the words, inaccessible areas, these regions were inaccessible until I fished with John Holley, a college friend who probably was the most dedicated crappie fisherman I ever have met. He would search for sandbars across the mouths of creeks and sloughs that no one could get into from the river.

"Hang on, John," he would say as he revved up his 25-horsepower Mercury motor and headed full throttle in his aluminum johnboat straight at a sandbar. Like the trick boat drivers at Cypress Gardens, Holley would hit the sandbar and jump his boat into those impossible-to-get-to sloughs or creeks. If the sandbar was unjumpable, Holley and I would get out of the boat and drag it and all our gear across the bar until we could get into the crappie-rich waters behind the shallow water. When I went fishing with Holley, I usually had on my work clothes, a pair of tennis shoes I didn't mind getting wet and made sure I ate my Wheaties before I left the house, because I knew we would have to work hard to catch crappie.

Bigger and better crappie often can be found in inaccessible areas.

A tactic that Holley used to find hidden fish was to force his boat in between trees and standing timber areas where other boats couldn't maneuver. Holley would spend an hour to an hour and a half working his boat into thick patches of standing timber just to get to the backside of these regions where no one else could fish and where he always seemed to locate the biggest and best crappie.

"Now, don't you tell anybody where we caught these fish," Holley always would say.

I never revealed where he took the crappie. Of course even if I had -- nobody in his right mind would have angled in some of the places that a boat had to be jumped, drug, pushed, squeezed and maneuvered into by Holley. I believe one of the keys to catching more and bigger crappie is to fish those hard-to-get-to places.

WHAT GORILLA TACKLE IS

In my good ole days, crappie were a survival food. We caught the fish to eat, to share with other college students and to cut down on our grocery bills. At that time, I figured that if a fish was three fingers wide, it would fry. We deliberately tried not to lose any fish that took our baits. As Holley said, "You play with fish when they are in the boat -- not when they're in the water."

127

That's why we purchased 16 foot canepoles and cut the ends so the poles would be about 12 feet long and resemble and have the flexibility of a pool cue. To this cane we attached 20-pound test line. If we had had Trilene XT available in those days, we would have used it because we needed the toughest line we could find due to the type of cover and terrain to which we exposed our fishing string. To the line, we affixed a quill cork.

"I want the crappie to be able to pull the cork down easily so it can take the bait into its mouth," Holley told me. "Then I can get a solid hook set. If the crappie is tangled in the brush, it will stay on the hook until I get it untangled."

A piece of shot lead and a gold Eagle Claw hook was tied on the end of the line. The hook was then straightened and bent back to its original position to weaken the wire so the hook would bend straight and pull free when, not if, it was hung in the cover.

"You want to be able to snatch the pole hard, straighten the hook and break it free from the cover without disturbing the crappie," Holley explained. "If you sit there, pull on your line and move the cover, you will run all the crappie off your hotspot. But if you will snatch the pole up hard and fast so the hook will straighten and come free instantly, you don't disturb as many fish. Even if you break a hook off, retying is better than running all the crappie in a school away from the cover you have located."

Holley used a flat bottom aluminum johnboat, because it would take a beating and get into small, tight spots where larger boats couldn't. He preferred a Mercury 25 outboard, because it had the power and speed to push his johnboat over sandbars, ditches and occasionally a beaver dam. When the prop hit mud or a log, the slip clutch would disengage and allow him to keep on motoring once he was over the obstacle.

HOW TO BAIT

John Holley was strictly a minnow fisherman. Since he always caught plenty of crappie on minnows, he never saw a reason to fish with jigs. In those days, jigs often cost more than minnows. Because of the way Holley angled and the

Flipping a lure or bait into heavy cover is a productive technique for many crappie fishermen.

areas where he was putting his baits, a Plano tackle box probably would not have held as many jigs as he lost daily.

"Don't give me any of those little minnows," he would always tell the man at the bait shop. "Little minnows catch small crappie. I want the largest crappie minnows you have because they will take the biggest crappie on the river."

Holley firmly believed that if you used big bait you caught big fish. After fishing with him for four years, I am convinced he was right -- at least for angling at that place, at that time and on the river we were fishing.

WHY TO USE A VERTICAL PRESENTATION

Flipping, a term in bass fishing, is a tactic that employs either a jig and pig or a jig and a worm. The angler swings the bait and allows it to fall vertically through heavy cover. When the technique of flipping first gained national attention in the bass fishing world, many anglers across the nation thought that presenting a bait vertically to the fish and through heavy cover was a new method. However, Holley was fishing this way for crappie 20 years ago.

"Bounce the minnow off the crappie's nose," Holley instructed. "Those crappie are holding in very thick cover. Many times you can fish all the way around a bush or a treetop and not get a bite. Most fishermen don't catch crappie because they aren't angling where the fish are. The angler who doesn't drop his bait into the heart of the bush won't catch them.

"I've found I can come right behind someone who has been fishing cover, fish that same cover and catch a limit of crappie when they haven't gotten a bite. You must put that minnow down through the structure, which means you have to get in close to the cover and drop the minnow through it. If you're going to fish in this type of heavy cover, you'll break hooks, poles and line and lose crappie. But I'd rather be fishing where the crappie are and catching and losing fish -- than fishing where the crappie aren't and not be getting a bite or losing any tackle."

HOW TO FISH WHERE THE CRAPPIE ARE

Holley was not an all-day treetop sitter. When the crappie quit biting in a spot, Holley stopped fishing there.

"You have to stay on the move if you are going to catch plenty of crappie," Holley said. "I may cover four miles of bank in a day or hit 20 different pieces of cover. If the fish are biting, I will catch them. If they are not, I will move to another place where they are biting."

Holley's philosophy of, "Fish where the crappie are," was demonstrated the first time I ever fished with him. He told me, "Why, I've caught as many as 20 to 30 crappie in a hole that didn't appear to be as big as a five-gallon can before and that may be the only hole where the crappie are biting. When you're fishing with me, and you catch a fish out of a spot, I'll fish there next. When I take a fish out of that hole, then you fish in there. We'll both catch more crappie, have more fun and spend less time looking for fish."

I soon adapted to Holley's philosophy. We might take 15 to 20 crappie out of a small area that would be just big enough for one quill cork to stand up in sometimes. Often, even after fishing all over the structure, we wouldn't get another bite except in that one place.

WHY WATCH THE WATER

"There are some big crappie in the back of that slough," Holley remarked as we paddled down the bank. "Watch the

130

shad on top. See the fish breaking the water? See the dead shad lying on top? I guarantee that's a big school of good-sized crappie in here."

John Holley was able to read the water and see the fish when they came to the surface to chase shad better than any angler with whom I ever have fished. Most of the time in the out-of-way places where we fished, the water was dead calm. Holley would take note of any disturbance on the water and usually be able to detect crappie -- even in open water when they were feeding on shad.

When we moved into a little pocket, Holley would tell me to, "Shallow up your cork. Your bait doesn't need to be more than two or three inches under the cork. The crappie are shallow and are looking up at the shad."

Once, in a small pocket of water, we took 25 of the biggest crappie I ever had caught anywhere at anytime in less than 30 minutes.

THE ADVANTAGES OF GORILLA TACTICS

* Most of the time you will be fishing for crappie that rarely see another bait.

* You usually catch bigger crappie in out-of-the-way places.

* Generally these hidden crappie holes that are hard to get to can be fished even on the windiest of days.

* Oftentimes little hidden pockets like Holley fished will stay more clear during muddy water conditions and will warm up first in the spring.

* An angler feels a certain pride when he is able to fish an area that very few other anglers can reach.

Although gorilla tactics are hard work, they most always have produced crappie.

131

- 15 -

WHAT WEIRD WAYS CATCH CRAPPIE

What do spiderwebs, blonde wig hair, goldfish, limbs hanging out over a lake and quart bleach bottles have in common? These are some of the newest, weird ways to catch crappie.

The saying that truth is stranger than fiction is often the rule rather than the exception in the world of crappie fishing. Who would have believed that a blonde lady's wig could enable Sterling Earhart of Mt. Julian, Tennessee, and Roger Jarvis of Nashville, Tennessee, to win $25,000 in the 1987 Crappiethon Classic by catching 20 crappie that weighed a total of 17.13 pounds? Who would have thought of tying jigs onto monofilament line and attaching that line to the limbs of bushes hanging out over the water so that when the wind blew, the bushes and the jigs moved, and crappie attacked the jigs?

Goldfish in a bowl are primarily used to entertain children. Or, if you're more sophisticated, different varieties of goldfish may be in your aquarium or pond at home. But Paul Johnson and Vernon Green, Sr., of McAlester, Oklahoma, buy goldfish to fish for crappie.

"We believe we catch bigger crappie on goldfish than we do on minnows," Johnson says.

"The goldfish also seem to live longer," Green explains. "And I think they're much easier for the crappie to see, especially in stained water."

There are some weird ways to catch crappie, but they may not be legal in some states. If you decide to try any of these tactics, be sure to check the regulations of the state where you plan to fish.

Jug fishing for catfish has been a tried and true technique for years. However, today many fishermen are utilizing quart bleach bottles to catch crappie. By tying monofilament on the necks of the jugs, they suspend either live minnows on hooks or 1/24- or 1/32-ounce crappie jigs on the lines and allow the jugs to blow across the mouths of creeks, river ledges and shallow water coves where the crappie may be spawning during the spring. The crappie take the jigs and tip up the jugs. Then the angler brings in the crappie.

All these weird ways to take crappie may not be legal in some states. If you decide to try any of these tactics, be sure to check the regulations of the state where you plan to fish.

The new weird methods of catching crappie are based on a single assumption, which according to Roger Jarvis is, "Crappie are just like humans in that they must eat every day somewhere. All you have to do to catch a crappie is find out where it wants to eat and feed it the bait it'll bite."

WIG HAIR AND FAKE FUR

Jarvis and Earhart have discovered that the bait crappie will bite best for them is either a 1/8- or a 1/16-ounce home-made jig with the skirt of the jig fashioned from either craft fur or wig hair.

"Artificial wig hair and fake fur will pulse as an angler reels a jig," Jarvis reports. "When the jig is moved forward, the hair or fur falls back against the hook. But if the jig is either slowed or stopped, the hair or fur will fluff up in the water. We believe this way is the most natural to present the bait to the fish."

When Earhart and Jarvis found out that the Crappiethon Classic would be held at Lake Harris in Hot Springs, Arkansas, one year, they knew they had to develop new strategies for taking papermouths, because the lake was deep and clear -- unlike most of the lakes in their native state of Tennessee. Their philosophy of crappie fishing -- you play like you practice -- evolved partially from Jarvis's playing football in college and the pros with the Washington Redskins under Vince Lombardi. Deep, clear water, post-spawn crappie fishing was a style of angling that neither man ever had pursued.

"We traveled to lakes away from home where the water was deep and clear and had very little structure," Jarvis says. "We learned that crappie in this type of water are much more spooky than stained water crappie. Anglers sitting over a bush top or brush top and trying to either jig or minnow fish often will cause clear water crappie to bury up deep in the bushes and not bite. Oftentimes trolling over the top of the crappie will spook the fish and make them hold tight to the cover. However, if you back your boat 15 to 20 yards away from the area you want to fish, cast the bait to the target and allow it to fall vertically, the crappie will move out of the brush and take the bait."

Jarvis and Earhart also have documented that pastel-colored jigs draw more strikes than bright colors in clear water.

"That's why we believe that blondes have more fun," Jarvis comments as he chuckles. "The wig hair jigs are deadly on papermouths. The dirty blonde color is a neutral color that seems to be more similar to the color of the baitfish in clear water that the crappie are accustomed to seeing."

But just getting the crappie to strike the bait is not enough to catch them.

"We've watched crappie in clear water suck a bait in and blow it out," Earhart observes. "So we realize we must do

135

something to make the crappie hold onto the bait longer. I think crappie fishermen may have to make a compromise to fish homemade jigs like ours. The best jig for crappie fishing available on the market is a bait like the Betts' jig with a lead head, a rubber body and a maribou feathered tail. I think when a crappie hits this kind of jig, that rubber body makes the crappie hold on longer.

"However, we feel the crappie will take our hair and fur jigs quicker and more often than they will the rubber jigs. But since they won't hold on as long to our homemade jigs, setting the hook is much harder. Therefore we dip our jigs in Berkley's Strike. I don't really care whether or not Strike attracts fish because I think that's the job of the jig. But we believe this substance does cause fish to hold onto the jigs a fraction of a second longer, which gives us more time to set the hooks.

"Also to really be an effective jig crappie fisherman, you mentally must see your bait from the time it hits the water and as it falls through the water and into the structure. By watching our lines, feeling and mentally seeing the baits and anticipating the strikes, we catch more crappie."

Although, traditionally, crappie fishermen have believed that crappie associate with structure, the latest crappie catching techniques emphasize moving away from the bank to invisible cover and fishing underwater structure.

"We have sunk hardwood trees in area lakes before to attract crappie, and we also fish creek and river channels and underwater brush just like bass anglers do," Earhart explains. "Instead of searching for crappie, we look for structure. Many times the crappie will be hiding under the structure or in it, and you won't be able to see them on the depthfinder. Some of the best catches of crappie we've made have been on structure where we couldn't see the fish on our depthfinder."

The correct bait presentation is critical to taking more crappie.

"If we're fishing any type of structure, we always anchor downwind of the structure, cast our jigs upwind past the target, and retrieve the lures with the wind through, over or by the structure," Earhart states. "Wind direction is important because the wind moves the plankton on which the

Wig hair may be able to produce good stringers of crappie like this for you.

baitfish feed. The baitfish follow the plankton, and the crappie eat the baitfish. If the crappie are accustomed to seeing the baitfish come from one direction, which is the same direction the wind is blowing, I don't think they will bite as readily if you present a jig from another direction."

Also, crappie anglers are catching plenty of fish that are suspended in the wintertime around deep, standing timber and in the springtime just prior to the spawn when the fish move up into the mouths of creeks.

"To catch suspended crappie, the depthfinder is all-important to success," Jarvis explains. "We look for the crappie in standing timber with the depthfinder and start pitching jigs

137

to them when we locate the fish. Once again, watching your line makes a difference in whether or not you catch the fish, because the crappie will attack the bait when the lure's falling. That's why we utilize 1/8- and 1/16- ounce jigs instead of 1/32- and 1/24-ounce crappie jigs. Sterling and I are convinced we can feel the heavier jigs as they fall better than the lighter jigs, which helps us know when to set the hooks."

SPIDERWEBBING

Yet another weird tactic for crappie catching is spiderwebbing, which is done by anglers who troll for crappie. The technique receives its name from the numerous poles jutting out from the boat and the lines trailing from these poles resembling a spiderweb. Oftentimes spiderwebbing means barely turning the trolling motor on and off to push the boat forward ever so slightly. Anglers who spiderweb may troll two or four pound test line, even up to six pound test line, with 1/24- or 1/32-ounce jigs attached.

In the states that permit anglers to use an unlimited number of rods to fish with, spiderwebbers may have 18 to 24 rods out from one boat at a time to cover 10 to 20 yards of water in one pass. These boats are rigged much like billfishing boats in saltwater. Flyrods or fiberglass crappie poles are used as outriggers. Shorter rods are trolled closer to the boat. Each line may have a different color of jig on it. After these jigs pass through a school of crappie, the color of jig that attracts the most fish will be put on all the lines.

The spider fisherman spots crappie on his depthfinder and slowly motors through the school with his lines trolling at the precise depth where the school is holding. The three factors that control the depth of the jigs are the size of the jig, the size of the line and the speed of the boat.

Through trial and error, spiderweb fishermen learn exactly at what depths their jigs are trolling. By increasing and decreasing the speed of their boats, they cause the jigs to either rise or fall in the water. Then the baits are trolled through the school at the exact depth where the crappie are holding. When 18 rods troll through a school of crappie simultaneously, if any or some of those jigs have a crappie encounter -- the result is much like the confusion and excite-

Spiderwebbing is most effective when crappie are suspended away from the bank. The technique receives its name from the numerous poles jutting out from the boat and the lines trailing from these poles resembling a spiderweb.

ment that happens when a skunk is released in a room full of school children.

The most productive time to catch crappie spiderwebbing is when the fish are suspended, which can occur at any time. However, large schools of crappie most often will suspend in the mouths of creeks just prior to the spawn where they're waiting for the temperature of the water to warm up enough to trigger their going to the banks to lay their eggs. Crappie also will suspend in the mouths of creeks just after the spawn when the water is still warm enough for the fish to be shallow and prior to the water temperature's heating up enough in the summertime to drive them back to the deep river and creek channel drop-offs.

Although crappie also will suspend in the winter in standing timber, these fish are hard to catch when you're spiderwebbing because of the difficulty in maneuvering a boat through the cover. Spiderwebbing also pays crappie dividends throughout the year when crappie concentrate above or close to the outer edges of structure. Anglers may be able to troll their jigs down close enough to the cover to catch the fish without allowing the jigs to get into the cover and break off.

Also minnow fishermen are trolling now by tying lead sinkers on the bottoms of their lines. Then about one to two feet above the sinkers, they attach one or two drop-lines off the main line and bait these with minnows. When using this tactic, minnow fishermen move their boats only slightly with their trolling motors to pull the minnows along creek and river channels. If their lines encounter brush, stumps or logs, the leads on the bottoms of the lines telegraph the structure encounter. Utilizing this tactic, often the hooks will not become lodged in the cover.

Trolling is not just a deep water tactic for live bait and jig fishermen. When the crappie come into the banks in the spring, and/or when they're holding shallow in the mouths of creeks or open water, fishermen often will use corks to suspend both minnows and/or jigs a foot to two feet under the surface and troll.

If you think spiderwebbing, angling with blonde wig hair and goldfish and fishing for crappie in the middle of a river where you can't see any visible cover is weird, most sportsmen will agree with you. The only reason anyone in his right mind employs these weird tactics is to catch more crappie.

- 16 -

HOW TO CHOOSE A CRAPPIE GUIDE

To become a master crappie fisherman, you don't simply wake up in the middle of the night and receive from the hand of the Almighty hundreds of years of crappie fishing knowledge. The best way to learn the masters' secrets of crappie fishing is to fish with the masters of the sport, read about the tactics they have developed and then apply those strategies in the field.

I like to fish with crappie fishing guides because ...

* they will find the most fish in any lake or river on any day,

* they know the best techniques for taking crappie on the body of water they fish regularly on the day I fish,

* they understand why the crappie are positioned on the structure the way they are,

* they are time and cost efficient, since I can catch more fish in a shorter time for less money with a guide than using any other method.

However, if you don't choose to employ a guide, you still can learn from their wisdom in this chapter and the others in the book.

"We're going to catch crappie today," Roger Gant of Corinth, Mississippi, said. "I can guarantee it. I've got these crappie trapped with a dam on the northern end of the lake so they can't swim upstream, a dam on the southern end of the lake to keep them from escaping downstream and banks on both sides of the lakes where they can't crawl out." I looked at Gant who was smiling. The lake where he had the crappie trapped was Pickwick Lake, one of the major reservoirs on the Tennessee River on the Mississippi/Tennessee/Alabama borders with miles and miles of shoreline and plenty of sloughs, bays and feeder creeks. "If I didn't think I could catch crappie, I'd stay at home," Gant explained. "We're gonna get 'em today."

Roger Gant breeds confidence in the anglers he takes fishing. His professionalism and system of guiding sets the standards for other guides to follow. When Gant picks you up to carry you on a fishing trip, he has a cellular phone in his vehicle for you to use to notify anyone you are leaving for the lake or coming in from the lake. He provides all the rods, reels and tackle you will need for a day of fishing. He allows you to catch the crappie rather than showing you how it's done. When the trip is over, he fillets your crappie, puts them in Ziploc bags and places them in an ice chest for your trip home.

"A good crappie guide should foresee the hassles associated with fishing and get rid of them," Gant advised. "When most anglers show up at a lake to crappie fish, they usually won't have the correct equipment or the most productive lures or bait for a successful trip. I think the guide's providing everything for the angler eliminates problems for his fisherman."

A problem you often encounter when employing a crappie guide is the guide catches all the fish. The guide knows how to fish to catch crappie but does not teach you how to use the same technique so you can be successful. Actually you are paying the guide to take the crappie you want to catch. Also, often the best technique to use on a lake may be the most difficult tactic to learn. A guide must be willing to change strategies or develop a new method to enable his clients to catch crappie.

"On Lake Weiss on the North Alabama/Georgia border, the crappie often will be holding on deep river and creek channels on stumprows," Sam Heaton of Gadsden, Alabama, one of the nation's leading crappie guides, reported. "One of the most effective ways to catch these fish is to cast 1/16- and 1/24-ounce jigs and retrieve them through the stumps near

Sam Heaton of Gadsden, Alabama, is one of the nation's leading crappie guides and not only knows how to find and catch crappie but knows how to teach others.

the bottom. However, anglers not accustomed to fishing with light lines and little jigs in heavy cover will spend all day breaking off jigs and becoming hung and frustrated."

To solve this problem, Heaton rigs up B & M poles with slip corks, which allow his clients to fish just over the stumps in the best depth of water to catch the crappie. "Using slip corks, poles and live minnows, each angler can fish two to three poles at a time while I move the boat along the breaklines and the underwater cover," Heaton mentions. "My clients can catch fish without fighting the frustration of getting hung."

HOW TO FIND AN OUT-OF-TOWN CRAPPIE GUIDE

How do you find a reputable crappie guide like Heaton or Gant who can make your fishing trip fun and rewarding?

If you don't live near the lake you want to fish, locating a good crappie guide who will put you on fish can be difficult. Probably the most efficient way to locate a knowledgeable and experienced crappie guide on any lake is to call the outdoor writer at the newspaper nearest the lake. Outdoor writers at local newspapers are charged with the responsibility of knowing the outdoor people in their areas as well as where to find the most up-to-date information on any particular day on any specific lake. Even if the writer is not certain which guide is best for you, he can give you the names of resource people to help you find the type of guide you prefer.

The next best source of information for locating a crappie guide is to call the chambers of commerce or tourism associations in or near the town where you plan to fish. These organizations should have the names and phone numbers of guides on all the lakes in their regions, since this is part of their job descriptions.

Also, call a sporting goods dealer and/or marina operator in the town nearest the lake because these stores have avid anglers passing through them every day. Even if they cannot list the guides on a particular lake, they should be able to give you the phone number of someone you can call who will have that information.

Or, you can contact either the police chief, the sheriff or the game and fish warden in the town or county where you plan to fish. Although most of us think of law enforcement officers as only knowing about crime and criminals, most law enforcement personnel are acquainted with most everyone and everything happening in their areas. Because they must have vast information bases to perform their jobs expertly and are available to serve people, often they will know who is the best crappie guide on any lake.

WHAT YOU SHOULD EXPECT OF A CRAPPIE GUIDE

When you hire a guide for the day, here are some standards by which to judge him.

1. A guide should have good equipment. His boat should be clean and well-kept and his trolling motor and outboard in good repair. He should have tackle and equipment on board for you to fish with, even if he requires you to bring your own equipment. If you break a rod or a pole, if you do not have the correct size of jigs or minnows, or if you show up with 10-pound test line when you should be fishing four

Even during bad weather, Charlie Ingram of Tom Mann's Fish World Guide Service helps his anglers find and take crappie.

pound test line, the guide should have equipment available for you to fish with to be successful that day.

2. The guide should know the lake and the most productive crappie locations. He should be able to put you in a position to catch fish at some time during the day. There are no excuses for your not catching crappie. According to Steve McCadams of Paris, Tennessee, a guide on Kentucky/Barkley lakes on the Kentucky/Tennessee border who has built more than 100 fishing reefs where his clients can catch fish, "I've got spots I can fish no matter which way the wind is blowing. I know of other sites I can fish under either muddy water or clear water conditions, deep water places for when the fish are deep and shallow water areas for when the crappie are shallow. I don't fish my spots every day, and I do let them rest. Then I can go to these sites and consistently produce fish for my clients. When people hire a crappie guide, they expect to

catch fish. My job is to do all in my power I can to ensure they do."

3. A crappie guide should have a pleasant attitude and make the trip fun and enjoyable for his clients. His job is not just to take his anglers to a place where they can catch crappie but also to provide an entertaining and fun day to go along with the fishing.

4. A crappie guide should be willing to teach youngsters and novices how to catch fish. He should be patient and train anglers in the skills required to be competent crappie fishermen. In most instances, you can learn more about how, where and when to catch crappie in one day of fishing with a guide than you can in eight weeks of trial and error crappie fishing.

5. A good crappie guide either will clean the fish or assist you in cleaning the fish, help you get your gear loaded and wave goodbye as you pull out of the marina. One of the tests of a quality crappie guide is what he does when the trip is over. Some guides want to take their pay and leave as quickly as possible, because they are tired and worn out like you are. They believe they have put in their time and that's all that should be required. However, oftentimes that extra 30 minutes spent in helping their clients at the end of a trip separates the great crappie guides from the average guides.

6. The crappie guide should be a constant teacher. His job is not only to allow you to catch fish but to teach you all he can about the sport of crappie fishing. Then you will return home with a nice mess of fish and a pleasant experience from a day on the water and also knowledge and the ability to catch more crappie the next time you go to the lake.

WHAT QUESTIONS YOU SHOULD ASK BEFORE THE TRIP

Problems can arise when you do not know what to expect from your guide. Ask these questions of a crappie guide before you consider taking a trip with him.

1. How much will the trip cost?
2. Does the price include the tip?
3. What amount do you usually expect for a tip if we have a good day?

146

One of the best ways to teach children to catch crappie and to show them the joys of crappie fishing is to take them fishing with a crappie guide.

4. What equipment is furnished on the trip?
5. What equipment is not furnished on the trip?
6. What time does the day of fishing begin?
7. What time does the day of fishing end?

8. If we catch a limit of crappie before our day is over, can we fish for other species?
9. Who cleans the fish?
10. Is there a charge for cleaning fish?
11. How many people are allowed to fish from your boat?
12. Do you fish with children?
13. Are you willing to help children learn to fish?
14. What are our chances of catching crappie?
15. What size crappie do you expect to catch?
16. Once we take the number of crappie we want to keep, can we continue to fish and release the crappie we catch?
17. Can you provide a list of names and phone numbers of other people who have fished with you?
18. Realistically, what are our chances of catching a limit of crappie or of catching big crappie?

Knowing the answers to these questions will make your crappie fishing experience much more fun and enjoyable, prevent any misunderstandings and give you a realistic picture of what to expect for a day of angling with your crappie guide.

THE ADVANTAGES OF FISHING WITH A GUIDE

When you fish with a guide, you spend more time angling and less time looking for crappie. You don't have to own a boat, a motor, a depthfinder and a large amount of equipment to fish. The guide can tell you what your chances for catching fish are before you reach the lake. The guide can call you when the crappie are biting. Too, he can tell you to stay at home when the fish are not biting, the weather is bad, or he knows you are going to have a miserable trip.

For dollars spent, the crappie guide can provide you, your family and your friends the most quality crappie fishing experience for the lowest cost. Once you determine the cost of the equipment you must have and the number of hours you must spend on a lake to find fish, you may decide that hiring a crappie guide will provide the best crappie fishing for you this year.

Larsen's Outdoor Publishing
FISHING & HUNTING
RESOURCE DIRECTORY

f you are interested in more productive ishing, hunting and diving trips, this nformation is for you!

Learn how to be more successful on your next outdoor enture from these secrets, tips nd tactics. Larsen's Outdoor ublishing offers informational- pe books that focus on how nd where to catch the most opular sport fish, hunt the most opular game or travel to pro- uctive or exciting destinations.

The perfect-bound, soft-cover ooks include numerous illustrative aphics, line drawings, maps and otographs. Many of our LIBRARIES e nationwide in scope. Others cover the ulf and Atlantic coasts from Florida Texas to Maryland and some foreign aters. One SERIES focuses on the top kes, rivers and creeks in the nation's most sited largemouth bass fishing state.

All series appeal to outdoors readers all skill levels. Their unique four- lor cover design, interior layout, uality, information content and onomical price makes these books ur best source of knowledge. Best of l, you will know how to be more uccessful in your outdoor deavors!!

HERE'S WHAT OUR READERS HAVE SAID!

"Larry, I'm ordering one book to give a friend for his birthday and your two new ones. I have all the BASS SERIES LIBRARY except one, otherwise I would have ordered an autographed set. I have followed your writings for years and consider them the best of the best!"
J. Vinson, Cataula, GA

"I am delighted with Frank Sargeant's Redfish Book. Please let me know when others in the Inshore Series will be available." J.A'Hern, Columbia, S.C.

Great Tips and Tactics For
The Outdoorsmen of the Nineties!

BASS SERIES LIBRARY
by Larry Larsen

(BSL1) FOLLOW THE FORAGE VOL. 1 - BASS/PREY RELATIONSHIP - Learn how to determine dominant forage in a body of water and you will consistently catch more and larger bass.

(BSL2) VOL. 2 BETTER BASS ANGLING TECHNIQUES - Learn why one lure or bait is more successful than others and how to use each lure under varying conditions.

(BSL3) BASS PRO STRATEGIES - Professional fishermen know how changes in pH, water level, temperature and color affect bass fishing, and they know how to adapt to weather and topographical variations. Learn from their experience. Your productivity will improve after spending a few hours with this compilation of techniques!

(BSL4) BASS LURES - TRICKS & TECHNIQUES - When bass become accustomed to the same artificials and presentations seen over and over again, they become harder to catch. You will learn how to modify your lures and rigs and how to develop new presentation and retrieve methods to spark the interest of largemouth!

(BSL5) SHALLOW WATER BASS - Bass spend 90% of their time in the shallows and you spend the majority of the time fishing for them in waters less than 15 feet deep. Learn productive new tactics that you can apply in marshes, estuaries, reservoirs, lakes, creeks and small ponds, and you'll likely triple your results!

(BSL6) BASS FISHING FACTS - Learn why and how bass behave during pre- and post-spawn, how they utilize their senses when active and how they respond to the environment, and you'll increase your bass angling success! By applying this knowledge, your productivity will increase for largemouth as well as redeye, Suwannee, spotted and other bass species!

(BSL7) TROPHY BASS - If you're more interested in wrestling with one or two monster largemouth than with a "panful" of yearlings, then learn what techniques and locations will improve your chances. This book takes a look at geographical areas and waters that offer better opportunities to catch giant bass. You'll also learn proven lunker bass-catching techniques for both man-made and natural bodies of water!

(BSL8) ANGLER'S GUIDE TO BASS PATTERNS - Catch bass every time out by learning how to develop a productive pattern quickly and effectively. "Bass Patterns" a reference source for all anglers, regardless of where they live or their skill level. Learn how to choose the right lure, presentation and habitat under various weather and environmental conditions!

(BSL9) BASS GUIDE TIPS - Learn secret techniques known only in a certain region or state that often work in waters all around the country. It's this new approach that usually results in excellent bass angling success. Learn how to apply what the country's top guides know!

Nine Great Volumes To Help You Catch More and Larger Bass!

LARSEN ON BASS SERIES

LB1) LARRY LARSON ON BASS TACTICS is the ultimate "how-to" book that focuses on proven productive methods. It is dedicated to serious bass anglers - those who are truly interested in learning more about the sport and in catching more and larger bass each trip. Hundreds of highlighted tips and drawings explain how you can catch more and larger bass in waters all around the country. This reference source by America's best known bass fishing writer will be invaluable to both the avid novice and expert angler!

BASS WATERS SERIES
by Larry Larsen

Take the guessing game out of your next bass fishing trip. The most productive bass waters in each Florida region are described in this multi-volume series, including boat ramps, seasonal tactics, water characteristics and much more. Both popular and overlooked locations are detailed with numerous maps and photos. The author has lived and fished extensively in each region of the state over the past 25 years.

BW1) GUIDE TO NORTH FLORIDA BASS WATERS - Covers from Orange Lake north and west. Includes Lakes Orange, Lochloosa, Talquin and Seminole, the St. Johns, Nassau, Suwannee and Apalachicola Rivers and many more of the region's best! You'll learn where bass bite in Keystone Lakes, Newnans Lake, St. Mary's River, Doctors Lake, Black Creek, Juniper Lake, Ortega River, Lake Jackson, Lake Miccosukee, Chipola River, Deer Point Lake, Blackwater River, Panhandle Mill Ponds and many more!

BW2) GUIDE TO CENTRAL FLORIDA BASS WATERS - Covers from Tampa/Orlando to Palatka. Includes Lakes George, Rodman, Monroe, Tarpon and the Harris Chain, the St. Johns, Oklawaha and Withlacoochee Rivers and many others! You'll find the best spots to fish in the Ocala Forest, Crystal River, Hillsborough River, Conway Chain, Homosassa River, Lake Minneola, Lake Weir, Lake Hart, Spring Runs and many more!

BW3) GUIDE TO SOUTH FLORIDA BASS WATERS - Covers from I-4 to the Everglades. Includes Lakes Tohopekaliga, Kissimmee, Okeechobee, Poinsett, Tenoroc and Blue Cypress, the Winter Haven Chain and many more! You'll learn where bass can be caught in Fellsmere Farm 13. Caloosahatchee River, Lake June-in-Winter, Lake Hatchineha, the Everglades, Lake Istokpoga, Peace River, Crooked Lake, Lake Osborne, St. Lucie Canal, lake Trafford, Shell Creek, Lake Marian, Myakka River, Lake Pierce, Webb Lake and many more!

> For more than 20 years, award-winning author Larry Larsen has studied and written about bass fishing. His angling adventures are extensive, from Canada to Honduras and from Cuba to Hawaii. He is Florida Editor for *Outdoor Life* and contributor to all major outdoor magazines.

OUTDOOR TRAVEL SERIES
by Larry Larsen and M. Timothy O'Keefe

Candid guides with inside information on the best charters, time of the year, and other important recommendations that can make your next fishing and/or diving trip much more enjoyable.

(OT1) FISH & DIVE THE CARIBBEAN - Vol. 1 Northern Caribbean, including Cozumel, Cayman Islands, The Bahamas, Jamaica, Virgin Islands and other popular destinations.Required reading for fishing and diving enthusiasts who want to know the most cost-effective means to enjoy these Caribbean islands. You'll learn how to select the best destination and plan appropriately for your specific interests.

(OT3) FISH & DIVE FLORIDA & The Keys - Includes in-depth information on where and how to plan a vacation to America's most popular fishing and diving destination. Special features include artificial reef loran numbers; freshwater springs/caves; coral reefs/barrier islands; gulf stream/passes; inshore flats/channels; and back country estuaries.

(OT2) FISH & DIVE THE CARIBBEAN - Vol. 2 - *COMING SOON!* Southern Caribbean, including Guadeloupe, Costa Rica, Venezuela, other destinations.

"Fish & Dive the Caribbean, Vol. 1" was one of four finalists in the Best Book Content Category of the National Association of Independent Publishers 1991 competition. Over 500 books were submitted by various U.S. publishers, including Simon & Schuster and Turner Publishing, Inc. Said the NAIP judges "An excellent source book with invaluable instructions for fishing or diving. Written by two nationally-known experts who, indeed, know what vacationing can be!"

DIVING SERIES
by M. Timothy O'Keefe

(DL1) DIVING TO ADVENTURE will inform and entertain novice and experienced divers alike with its in-depth discussion of how to get the most enjoyment from diving and snorkeling. Aimed at divers around the country, the book shows how to get started in underwater photography, how to use current to your advantage, how to avoid seasickness, how to dive safely after dark, and more. Special sections detail how to plan a dive vacation, including live-aboard diving.

M. Timothy O'Keefe was editor of the first major dive travel guidebook published in the U.S. The award-winning author writes for numerous diving, travel and sportfishing publications.

COASTAL FISHING GUIDES

FG1) FRANK SARGEANT'S SECRET SPOTS - Tampa Bay to Cedar Key - A unique "where-to" book of detailed secret spots for Florida's finest saltwater fishing. This guide book describes little-known honeyholes and tells exactly how to fish them. Prime seasons, baits and lures, marinas and dozens of detailed maps of the prime spots are included. A comprehensive index helps the reader to further pinpoint productive areas and tactics.

FG2) FRANK SARGEANT'S SECRET SPOTS -Southwest Florida
COMING SOON!!

INSHORE SERIES

by Frank Sargeant

(IL1) THE SNOOK BOOK-"Must" reading for anyone who loves the pursuit of this unique sub-tropic species. Every aspect of how you can find and catch big snook is covered, in all seasons and all waters where snook are found.

(IL2) THE REDFISH BOOK-Packed with expertise from the nation's leading redfish anglers and guides, this book covers every aspect of finding and fooling giant reds. You'll learn secret techniques revealed for the first time. After reading this informative book, you'll catch more redfish on your next trip!

(IL3) THE TARPON BOOK-Find and catch the wily "silver king" along the Gulf Coast, north through the mid-Atlantic, and south along Central and South American coastlines. Numerous experts share their most productive techniques.

(IL4) THE TROUT BOOK -Jammed with tips from the nation's leading trout guides and light tackle anglers. For both the old salt and the rank amateur who pursue the spotted weakfish, or seatrout, throughout the coastal waters of the Gulf and Atlantic.

Frank Sargeant is a renown outdoor writer and expert on saltwater angler. He has traveled throughout the state and Central America in pursuit of all major inshore species. Sargeant is Outdoor Editor of the Tampa Tribune and a Senior Writer for *Southern Saltwater* and *Southern Outdoors* magazines.

HUNTING LIBRARY

by John E. Phillips

(DH1) MASTERS' SECRETS OF DEER HUNTING - Increase your deer hunting success significantly by learning from the masters of the sport. New information on tactics and strategies for bagging deer is included in this book, the most comprehensive of its kind.

(DH2) THE SCIENCE OF DEER HUNTING - Covers why, where and when a deer moves and deer behavior. Find the answers to many of the toughest deer hunting problems a sportsman ever encounters!

(TH1) MASTERS' SECRETS OF TURKEY HUNTING - Masters of the sport have solved some of the most difficult problems you will encounter while hunting wily longbeards with bows, blackpowder guns and shotguns. Learn the 10 deadly sins of turkey hunting and what to do if you commit them.

FISHING LIBRARY

(CF1) MASTERS' SECRETS OF CRAPPIE FISHING by John E. Phillips - Learn how to make crappie start biting again once they have stopped, how to select the color of jig to catch the most and biggest crappie, how to find crappie when a cold front hits and how to catch them in 100-degree heat as well as through the ice. Unusual but productive crappie fishing techniques are included. **Whether you are a beginner or a seasoned crappie fisherman, this book will improve your catch!**

OUTDOOR ADVENTURE LIBRARY

by Vin T. Sparano, Editor-in-Chief, <u>Outdoor Life</u>

(OA1) HUNTING DANGEROUS GAME -It's a special challenge to hun dangerous game - those dangerous animals that hunt back! Live the adventur of tracking a rogue elephant, surviving a grizzly attack, facing a charging Cap buffalo and driving an arrow into a giant brown bear at 20 feet. These classi tales will make you very nervous next time you're in the woods!

(OA2) GAME BIRDS & GUN DOGS - A unique collection of stories abou hunters, their dogs and the upland game and waterfowl they hunt. These tale are about those remarkable shots and unexplainable misses. You will rea about good gun dogs and heart-breaking dogs, but never about bad dog because there's no such animal.

LARSEN'S OUTDOOR PUBLISHING

CONVENIENT ORDER FORM

ASS SERIES LIBRARY ($11.95 ea.
or $79.95 for autographed set)
_ 1. Better Bass Angling Vol 1
_ 2. Better Bass Angling Vol 2
_ 3. Bass Pro Strategies
_ 4. Bass Lures Tricks/Techniques
_ 5. Shallow Water Bass
_ 6. Bass Fishing Facts
_ 7. Trophy Bass
_ 8. Bass Patterns
_ 9. Bass Guide Tips

ISHORE LIBRARY ($11.95 ea.
or $35.95 for autographed set)
_ IL1. The Snook Book
_ IL2. The Redfish Book
_ IL3. The Tarpon Book
_ IL4. The Trout Book

OASTAL FISHING GUIDES
($14.95)
_ FG1.Sargeant's Secret Spots -
Tampa Bay/Cedar Key

BASS WATERS SERIES ($14.95 ea.
or $37.95 autographed set)
___ BW1. Guide/North Fl. Bass Waters
___ BW2. Guide/Cntrl Fl. Bass Waters
___ BW3. Guide/South Fl. Bass Waters

LARSEN ON BASS SERIES ($14.95)
___LB1. Larry Larsen on Bass Tactics

OUTDOOR TRAVEL SERIES
($13.95 ea.)
___ OT1. Fish & Dive The Caribbean
___ OT3. Fish & Dive Florida/ Keys

DIVING SERIES ($11.95)
___ DL1. Diving to Adventure

HUNTING LIBRARIES/FISHING
LIBRARIES ($11.95 ea.)
___ DH1. Mstrs' Secrets/ Deer Hunting
___ DH2. Science of Deer Hunting
___ TH1. Mstrs' Secrets/ Turkey Hunting
___ OA1.Hunting Dangerous Game!
___ OA2.Game Birds & Gun Dogs
___ CF1. Mstrs' Secrets /Crappie Fishing

> **BIG SAVINGS!**
> 2-3 books, discount 10%
> 4 or more books, discount 20%

> **FOREIGN ORDERS**
> Please send check in U.S. funds
> drawn on a U.S. bank and add $2
> per book for airmail rate

ALL PRICES INCLUDE POSTAGE/HANDLING

o. of books _____ x $_____ each = $_____
o. of books _____ x $_____ each = $_____
o. of books _____ x $_____ each = $_____
Multi-book Discount (%) $_____

OTAL ENCLOSED (check or money order) $_____

AME_____ADDRESS_____

ITY_____STATE_____ZIP_____

Send check or Money Order to: **Larsen's Outdoor Publishing, Dept. RD93**
2640 Elizabeth Place, Lakeland, FL 33813

e'll send this brochure free to a friend:
iend's name_____Address_____
ty_____State_____Zip_____

WRITE US!

If our books have helped you be more productive in your outdoor endeavors, we'd like to hear from you! Let us know which book or series has strongly benefited you and how it has aided your success or enjoyment. We'll listen.

We also might be able to use the information in a future book. Such information is also valuable to our planning future titles and expanding on those already available.

Simply write to Larry Larsen, Publisher, Larsen's Outdoor Publishing, 2640 Elizabeth Place, Lakeland, FL 33813.

We appreciate your comments!

Larry Larsen

OUTDOOR SPORTS SHOWS, CLUB SEMINARS and IN-STORE PROMOTIONS

Over the course of a year, most of our authors give talks, seminars and workshops at trade and consumer shows, expos, book stores, fishing clubs, department stores and other places. Please try to stop by and say hi to them. Bring your book by for an autograph and some information on secret new hot spots and methods to try. At these events, we always have our newest books, so come and check out the latest information. If you know of an organization that needs a speaker, contact us for information about fees. We can be reached at 813-644-3381. At our autograph parties, we talk "outdoors" and how to enjoy it to the fullest!

Save Money On Your Next Outdoor Book!

Because you've purchased a Larsen's Outdoor Publishing
Book, you can be placed on our growing list of
preferred customers.

You can receive special discounts on our wide selection of
Outdoor Libraries and Series, written by our
expert authors.

PLUS...

Receive Substantial Discounts for Multiple Book Purchases

AND...

Advance notices on upcoming books!

Yes, put my name on your mailing list to receive

1. Advance notice on upcoming outdoor books
2. Special discount offers

Name_____

Address_____

City, State, Zip_____

Additional books from our friends at Night Hawk Publications

___FISH & FIXINGS COOKBOOK - by John & Denise Phillips
When you take more crappie after reading The Masters' Secrets of Crappie Fishing, you'll need this well-researched cookbook by the authors who have more than 60 years' combined experience in caring for and preparing fish. This cookbook contains more than 125 delicious recipes for grilling, broiling, baking and frying saltwater and freshwater fish as well as more than 125 recipes for side dishes and numerous tips on handling fresh and frozen fish. **$14 each (includes postage/handling)**

___DEER & FIXINGS COOKBOOK- by John & Denise Phillips
Prepare venison, a heart-smart meat with fewer calories, fat or cholesterol but more protein than chicken, in a wide variety of delicious dishes. Besides information on field and home care of venison, the cookbook features more than 100 proven venison recipes and more than 100 recipes for side dishes to accompany venison. **$14 each (includes postage/handling)**

___OUTDOOR LIFE'S COMPLETE TURKEY HUNTING
by John E. Phillips - Includes tactics from more than 35 of the best turkey hunters across the nation for hunting gobblers, with 180 drawings/photos. **$27.95 each (includes postage/handling)**

___DOUBLEDAY'S TURKEY HUNTER'S BIBLE
by John E. Phillips - This widely researched book contains information on every facet of turkey hunting for both novice and advanced hunters. **$14.50 each (includes postage/handling)**

___TURKEY TACTICS by John E. Phillips
Part of the North American Hunting Club's library, this comprehensive book covers the biology and habits of the wild turkey and gives a vast array of strategies for bagging them. **$21.00 each (includes postage/handling)**

Send check or money order to:
Night Hawk Publications
P.O. Drawer 375, Fairfield, AL 35064
Mastercard or Visa orders, call 800/627-4295

About The Artist

Fifty-three-year-old Willie Logan of Northport, Alabama, has been painting, drawing and "doing art" all his life, but has been professional involved with artwork for the past 30 years. Specializing also in painting oil portraits and landscapes, Logan is best known for his wildlife paintings and his life-size wood sculptures of wildlife. Logan's commissioned work for his sculptures and paintings have earned wide recognition across the south, where his work has been featured on numerous television programs and newspaper articles.

Contact Willie Logan at 14742 Highway 43 North, Northport, AL 35476; phone 205/339-1422 or 330-4804 for further information.